CONTENTS

TENNIS

NORTH WEST KENT COLLEGE
DARTFORD · GRAVESEND

Gravesend Campus Library

Direct Telephone Line : (01322) 629615

This book has been issued for four weeks.
Fines will be charged for late returns.

Human Kinetics

Library of Congress Cataloging-in-Publication Data

Brown, Jim, 1940-
   Tennis : steps to success / Jim Brown. -- 2nd ed.
     p. cm. -- (Steps to success activity series)
   ISBN 0-87322-555-4 (pbk.)
     1. Tennis. I. Title. II. Series.
   GV995.B6924   1995
   796.342'2--dc20   94-43319
                                    CIP

ISBN: 0-87322-555-4

Developmental Editor: Judy Patterson Wright, PhD; **Assistant Editors:** Julie Marx Ohnemus, John Wentworth, and Ed Giles; **Copyeditor:** Rebecca Tavernini; **Proofreader:** Kathy Bennett; **Typesetters:** Tara Welsch, Ruby Zimmerman, and Kathy Boudreau-Fuoss; **Text Layout:** Tara Welsch; **Text Design:** Keith Blomberg; **Cover Design:** Jack Davis; **Photographer (cover):** Wilmer Zehr; **Illustrator:** Keith Blomberg; **Printer:** United Graphics

Instructional Designer for the Steps to Success Activity Series: Joan N. Vickers, EdD, University of Calgary, Calgary, Alberta, Canada

Human Kinetics books are available at special discounts for bulk purchase. Special editions or book excerpts can also be created to specification. For details, contact the Special Sales Manager at Human Kinetics.

Printed in the United States of America   10 9 8

Human Kinetics
Web site: www.humankinetics.com

United States: Human Kinetics
P.O. Box 5076
Champaign, IL 61825-5076
800-747-4457
e-mail: humank@hkusa.com

Canada: Human Kinetics
475 Devonshire Road, Unit 100
Windsor, ON N8Y 2L5
800-465-7301 (in Canada only)
e-mail: orders@hkcanada.com

Europe: Human Kinetics
Units C2/C3 Wira Business Park
West Park Ring Road
Leeds LS16 6EB, United Kingdom
+44 (0)113 278 1708
e-mail: hk@hkeurope.com

Australia: Human Kinetics
57A Price Avenue
Lower Mitcham, South Australia 5062
08 8277 1555
e-mail: liahka@senet.com.au

New Zealand: Human Kinetics
P.O. Box 105-231, Auckland Central
09-523-3462
e-mail: hkp@ihug.co.nz

PREFACE

Learning to play tennis isn't easy. For most people it takes practice, patience, and, in most cases, professional instruction. You can provide the first two, and with this book, a good tennis teacher can be your instructional partner to help you play the game soon and well.

This second edition of *Tennis: Steps to Success* has 12 steps that allow you to move from the basic skills into game-like situations. There are more than 100 drills in this book to help you improve your skills, practice effectively, and record your progress. Both mental and physical skills are incorporated so that you can use all of your resources to improve your game. Suggested ways to increase or decrease the difficulty of the drills let you self-pace your progress to match your ability level. The sections titled "Success Stoppers" identify typical problems experienced by tennis players during learning and provide specific suggestions for correcting those problems. These suggestions can often be applied either during practice or a game.

The emphasis of my teaching and of *Tennis: Steps to Success* is to get players involved in game-like situations as soon as possible. Strategy has been incorporated into the drills and summarized for singles and doubles play. Lengthy explanations and standing in lines are out. Rallying with a partner across the net minutes after the beginning of the first lesson is not only in—it is expected. Whether it's practice, private lessons, group sessions, or school classes, you should be playing, hitting, tossing to others, or picking up balls almost all of the time.

The sequence of the 12 steps is not random. It has been carefully developed over a long playing and teaching career. Each step prepares you for the next one and moves you closer to becoming the best tennis player your talent and time will allow.

Racket handling skills and moving around the court precede learning to hit forehands and backhands. Beginning punch serves come before advanced, full-swing motions. Playing near the net and hitting simple volleys will prepare you for aggressively winning points with advanced volleys later on. Don't worry about more sophisticated shots like lobs, smashes, and half volleys yet. There is plenty to do before that.

The best news is that there is no timetable for your personal tennis learning program. Go as fast as you want to, as long as you touch all of the bases along the way. Don't become frustrated—some players may hit perfect forehands with very little instruction, but others struggle with the stroke for a lifetime.

Enjoy tennis, but don't underestimate it. Learning to play is not like riding a bicycle. Just because you do something once does not mean you can do it every time or in every situation. It's one thing to execute perfect groundstrokes when an instructor or friend feeds you every shot on one bounce and waist high. It is quite another to hit those shots against a practice partner or opponent who cannot or does not want to be so accommodating. That's what makes tennis challenging and fun at the same time.

Although *Tennis: Steps to Success* can be a do-it-yourself package, you don't have to master every skill before playing and enjoying yourself. As soon as you can hit balls back and forth across the net and punch a serve in to get a point started, you are ready to play tennis. If you wait for perfection, you will miss the fun.

Writing this book was a team effort. Arlene and Matthew Brown are good writers, editors, listeners, lab subjects, and computer problem-solvers. Their support made *Tennis: Steps to Success* and all of my writing possible, and I thank them for it.

THE STEPS TO SUCCESS STAIRCASE

Get ready to climb a staircase—one that will lead you to become a great tennis player. You cannot leap to the top; you get there by climbing one step at a time. Each of the 12 steps you will take is an easy transition from the one before. The first few steps of the staircase provide a foundation—a solid foundation of basic skills and concepts. As you progress further, you will learn how to connect groups of these seemingly isolated skills. Practicing common combinations of tennis skills will give you the experience you need to begin making natural and accurate decisions on the tennis court. You will learn to choose the proper stroke to match your various tennis needs—whether for quickness, power, deception, or just fun. As you near the top of the staircase, the climb will become easier, and you'll find that you have developed a sense of confidence in your tennis abilities that makes further progress a real joy.

Familiarize yourself with this section as well as "The Game of Tennis: Change Is the Name" and the "Equipment: Choose Your Weapons" sections for an orientation and help in setting up your practice sessions around the steps.

Follow the same sequence each step (chapter) of the way:

1. Read the explanations of what is covered in the step, why the step is important, and how to execute or perform the step's focus, which may be a basic skill, concept, or tactic, or a combination of the three.

2. Follow the numbered illustrations showing exactly how to position your body to execute each basic skill successfully. There are three general phases to each skill: preparation (getting into a starting position), execution (performing the skill that is the focus of the step), and follow-through (recovering to starting position). These are your "Keys to Success."

3. Look over the descriptions in the "Success Stoppers" section of common errors that may occur and the recommendations for how to correct them.

4. Read the directions, the Success Goal, and the Success Check items for each drill. Practice accordingly, record your score in the blank, and compare your results with the Success Goal. You need to meet the Success Goal of each drill before moving on to the next one, because most of the drills are arranged in an easy-to-difficult progression. This sequence is designed specifically to help you achieve your skills through repetition and purposeful practice. Pace yourself by adjusting the drills to either decrease or increase the difficulty, depending on which best fits your ability.

5. As soon as you can reach the Success Goal for one step you are ready for a qualified observer—such as your teacher, coach, pro, or trained partner—to evaluate your basic skill technique with the Keys to Success items. This is an evaluation of your basic technique or form, which can enhance your performance.

6. Repeat these procedures for each of the 12 Steps to Success. Then rate yourself according to the directions for "Rating Your Progress."

   Good luck on your step-by-step journey to developing your tennis skills, building confidence, experiencing continuous progress, and having fun!

Key

- - - →	= path of ball		⊕	= tennis ball bounce
───→	= path of player		▨	= box target
A, B, C, D	= players		▧	= target area
S	= server		1,2,3	= order of hits
R	= receiver			

THE GAME OF TENNIS: CHANGE IS THE NAME

Tennis has changed drastically in a relatively short period of time. When Walter Wingfield received a British patent for lawn tennis in 1874, he could not have predicted what the game would be like today.

Not long ago, tennis was a game played mostly by rich men who belonged to exclusive clubs. Although club tennis is still strong, people of all socioeconomic classes now play, and in the United States 60% of them play free of charge on public courts. When the United States Lawn Tennis Association (now the United States Tennis Association) extended its "protective wing" to women in 1889, tennis became a respectable sport for both sexes. Today, 45% of all players are women.

The 22 million Americans who play tennis at least once a year now range in age from the 8-and-under group to those over 75 years of age. Most of them are amateurs who play for fun with friends, in tournaments, on teams, and in leagues throughout the country.

Tennis in the '90s

Once tennis was played by amateurs only. Now world-class players often turn professional during their teens. Open tennis, in which professionals compete with amateurs, started in the 1960s. Tennis remains one of the few sports in which this happens regularly.

Television has been responsible for many of the changes in tennis. The number of players, products, and programs increased almost simultaneously with the growing number of tennis events shown on television. Now major events like Wimbledon (played in England) and the U.S. Open attract audiences of millions around the world.

The players and advertisements seen on television have had a significant economic impact on companies selling equipment and accessories in pro shops, specialty shops, and sporting goods stores. However, the impact is cyclical and varies from country to country. During the 1970s and early 1980s, the amount of tennis programming on American television increased dramatically. Retailers promoted rackets, clothes, and shoes to huge television audiences. A company could introduce a new men's shirt by having a player under contract wear the shirt in the finals of Wimbledon or the U.S. Open. The exposure would produce worldwide demand for the shirt the following day.

Now, tennis is televised less during prime time in the United States, but more in Europe, particularly on the German network, EuroSport. The resulting influence on tennis-related sales in Europe is significant, and manufacturers are spending more advertising dollars in countries other than the United States. The bottom line is, the more televised tennis matches and commercials, the greater the effect on sales of rackets, clothes, shoes, and accessories. The less television time devoted to tennis, the smaller the chance that the public is influenced by players and advertisements.

Tennis has also been changed by technology. Once, courts were made only of grass, clay, or concrete. Now, they are made of colorful synthetic products with made-to-order surfaces. Tennis rackets have gone from wood to high modulus graphite, boron, fiberglass, and Kevlar. The size of racket heads started at 60 to 70 square inches, ranged up to jumbo-size 116-plus-inch models, and settled down to midsize and oversize frames of 90 to 110 square inches. The width of tennis rackets changed from narrow to widebody and back again.

Finally, tennis instruction has changed. During the first two thirds of the century, interest was not high enough to support many teaching professionals. Now, tennis pros, teachers, coaches, camps, courses, and clinics exist throughout the country. Organizations and businesses that train and certify people to become professionals have also proliferated.

If you want to become more involved in the game and live in the United States, join the United States Tennis Association (USTA), 70 West Oak Lane, White Plains, NY 10604 (914-696-7000). USTA members can play in sponsored tournaments, receive tennis publications, get professional instruction, and obtain other benefits of belonging to an organization with hundreds of thousands of members.

National organizations similar to the USTA exist in almost every country in the world and provide the same kinds of benefits and services. Every national tennis association is a member of the International Tennis Federation (ITF), with headquarters in London, near Wimbledon.

Playing a Game, Set, Match

Singles is a *match* between two players; doubles is a match between four players—two on each team; and mixed doubles is a match pairing a man and woman on one team against a man and woman on the other team.

After a brief warm-up, the players decide, by spinning a racket or flipping a coin, who will serve first and on which end of the court they will begin the match. The ball is put into play by a serve, and the point is played out. *Points* are won when the opponent hits into the net, outside the boundary lines, or does not hit the ball before it bounces twice. After the serve, players may hit the ball before or after it has bounced on the court.

One player serves an entire *game*, which may last from 4 points to an indefinite number of points. The server alternately serves from the right and left sides of the baseline to the receiver, who also moves back and forth from right to left to return the serve. A *set* is won when one player has won at least 6 games and is ahead by at least 2 games. The final score in a set might be 6-0, 6-1, 6-2, 6-3, 6-4, 7-5, 8-6, etc.

A player wins a match by winning 2 out of 3 or 3 out of 5 sets. When time is limited, pro sets might constitute a match. A pro set is won by the player who wins at least 8 games and who is ahead by at least 2 games. Players change ends of the court when the total number of games played in a set is an odd number.

In most matches, players are responsible for keeping their own score and for calling their opponent's shots in or out of bounds. No sound from a player means the shot is "in" and play continues. Shots that hit the lines are considered in. Shouting "out" means the ball landed outside the boundary line and the point is over. In some tournament competition, an umpire may stand or sit near the net, call out the score, and settle disputes on close shots. At higher levels of the game, linespersons are positioned to make line calls. See Diagram 1 to learn the lines and areas of the court.

A *match* may also refer to competition between two teams representing schools, clubs, or other groups. Within a match there are sets, games, and points.

A tennis *tournament* involves teams or individuals competing against other teams or individuals in a series of matches. A high school or college team, for example, may enter a single elimination tournament, meaning after one team loses they are eliminated from competition. The U.S. Open and Wimbledon are examples of single elimination tournaments for the best players in the world. A double elimination tournament means a team

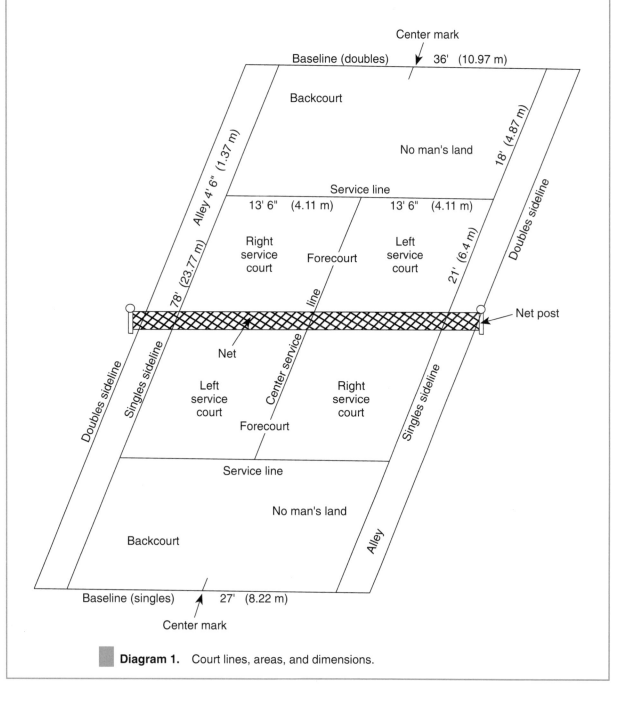

Diagram 1. Court lines, areas, and dimensions.

that loses two matches is out. A round robin tournament involves a team competing against all of the teams entered in that tournament; the team with the best overall win-loss record wins the tournament. Individuals can also enter the same kinds of tournaments.

Singles Rules

Players take all practice shots before the match begins. Warm-ups are usually limited to 5 minutes. The player who wins the racket spin or coin toss may choose to serve, to receive, or on which side of the court to play the first game. The winner also has the option to make the other player choose first. The other player gets to choose whatever the winner hasn't chosen—serve, receive, or side of court. Read the Singles Strategy chapter to learn more about these options.

The server stands behind the baseline, to the right of the extended center mark and inside the singles sideline, facing the net for the first point. When the opponent is ready, the server has two chances to put the ball into play by tossing it up and hitting it into the service court across the net and diagonally opposite from the baseline serving position. The server cannot step on or beyond the baseline before striking the ball.

The receiver is ready if an attempt is made to return the serve. The receiver can stand anywhere, but must let the ball bounce after the serve before returning it. After each point, the server alternates between the left and right sides of the center mark to serve. If a served ball hits the top of the net and goes into the proper court, it is called a "let" and the serve is repeated.

You can win points if your opponent

- fails in both attempts to serve the ball into the proper court,
- hits the ball outside of the proper boundary lines,
- hits the ball into the net,
- lets the ball bounce twice before returning it,
- reaches over the net to hit a ball before it has bounced,
- throws the racket and hits the ball,
- touches the net with his or her body or racket while the ball is in play,
- deliberately carries or catches the ball on the racket strings,
- does anything to hinder the opponent in making a shot,
- touches the ball with anything other than the racket during play, or
- touches or catches the ball during play, even if standing outside the court.

Doubles Rules

The server may stand anywhere behind the baseline between the center mark and the doubles sideline. The four players take turns serving an entire game. The order of serving stays the same throughout the set. In a game of AC versus BD, A serves, then B, then C, then D. Receivers decide who will receive serves on the right and left sides, respectively, and maintain that order throughout the set. Other rules described for singles apply to doubles, except that after the serve, the alleys between the singles and doubles sidelines are in play.

Scoring

The server's score is always given first. Points are love (0), 15 (the 1st point won by either player), 30 (the 2nd point), 40 (the 3rd point), and game (the 4th point). If the players are tied at 3 or more points during a game, the score is called "deuce." After deuce, when the server goes ahead by 1 point, the score is *ad in* or *advantage server*. If the receiver scores a point, it's *ad out*. A player must win 2 consecutive points after deuce in order to win that game. If not, the score goes back to deuce.

No-Ad Scoring

No-ad scoring was introduced to simplify the method of keeping score and to reduce the length of matches. It is much easier for casual fans and even for players to learn and remember a simple 1-2-3 system than the 15-30-40-deuce-ad method. Since no-ad scoring eliminates the requirement of having to win games by at least 2 points, the overall length of tennis matches can be reduced considerably. High school and college matches are usually played on unlighted courts after school and before dark. No-ad scoring allows matches to be completed during daylight. Also, tournaments with large numbers of players, a restricted amount of time, and limited court space frequently use this method of score keeping.

The disadvantage of no-ad scoring is that the system penalizes the well-conditioned athlete. The player with good endurance can use longer games and sets to wear down an opponent. This doesn't happen as much in no-ad scoring. Because no game will last more than 7 points, it may be possible for a player who gets a good start to gain an edge that cannot be overcome in a short match.

Here is how the system works. The first player to win 4 points wins the game. Points are 1, 2, 3, and game. When the score is tied at 3-3, the next point determines that game. At 3-3, the receiver chooses to receive the serve from either the right or left side.

Tiebreakers

Tiebreakers were incorporated into the scoring system mainly as a result of television. With traditional scoring, the length of matches is unpredictable. Sets have lasted for 30 and 40 games, making it difficult to sell advertising time and to manage programming schedules. Tie-break games were introduced so a 6-6 set could end quickly.

Tiebreakers work like this: In a 12-point tiebreak, the player or team that wins 7 points and is ahead by at least 2 points wins the game and that set. The score is called out as 1, 2, 3, 4, etc., throughout the game. A final tie-break score might be 7-0, 7-1, 7-2, 7-3, 7-4, 7-5, 8-6, 9-7, etc.

The singles player (or the player on the doubles team) whose turn it is to serve serves the 1st point from the right court. The opponent is the server for the 2nd and 3rd points, and after that, each player serves alternately for 2 consecutive points until the winner of the game and set has been decided. The second server serves the 2nd and 3rd points from the left and right courts, respectively, and this alternating continues until the tie-break game is completed. See Diagram 2 for the rotation of servers and their positions.

Players change ends of the court after every 6 points and at the end of the tiebreaker. The player or team who served first in the tie-break game receives the serve in the first game of the next set.

Unwritten Rules

Because most tennis matches are played on the honor system without officials, a few unwritten rules exist for players and spectators.

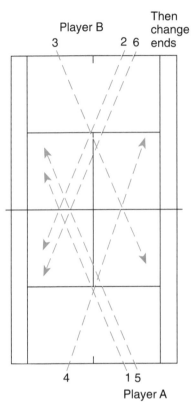

Player B

3   2 6

Then change ends

4   1 5

Player A

Diagram 2. Tie-break serving procedures.

- If you ask someone to play a match, provide the tennis balls yourself.
- Take all practice serves before the first game begins, not when it is your turn to serve the first time.
- In unofficiated matches, keep your own score. It is a good idea for the server to announce the score prior to each point.
- Each player is responsible for calling balls out on his or her side of the court. If you are in doubt, the shot is good. Never say, "Take two," just because you are not sure of whether a shot was in or out.
- Don't ask spectators if a ball is in or out. It's not their business and they are not in a position to make a call, anyway.
- Play "in" shots. Immediately and loudly call all others "out." Never call shots "in."
- If a dispute arises about a line call, try to settle the argument with your opponent. If that doesn't work, ask for an umpire.
- If a loose ball on or behind the court interferes with concentration or becomes a safety hazard, call a let immediately and replay the point.
- If there is an unusual delay between the first and second serves, allow your opponent to "take two"—start the serving sequence over.
- Don't shout or distract your opponent in any way during a match. It is not only improper, it's against the rules. It is also immature to groan, complain, curse, or verbally abuse yourself or others during a match.
- Avoid walking behind a court during a point. Tennis players spend as much time between the baseline and the fence as they do inside the lines. Stay out of their way and their vision.

- When returning a stray ball to its court, wait until the point has been completed. Immediately returning the ball interferes with play.
- If one of your tennis balls rolls onto an adjacent court, wait for play on that court to stop before asking for your ball to be returned. "Thanks, court two," is one polite way to ask for help.
- Shake hands with your opponent at the net after a match.
- If you are a spectator, hold your applause or cheers until a point has been completed. Tennis players react to sound (as in "out" or "fault") and may stop a point if your noise is interpreted as a line call.
- Applaud or cheer well-played points and winning shots rather than errors made by a friend's opponent.

Warm-Up and Cooldown

The most common but least effective way to warm up is to hit balls. It is one way to get started, but with this method players have a tendency not to exercise all of their muscles until actual play or difficult drills begin. When you do not warm up properly, the chance of injuries is greater. A good warm-up period should prepare your body for strenuous activity without being tiring. Look at the warm-up as having two phases—a warm-up period and a time to stretch. Then you can practice hitting specific shots. After practice or play take time to cool down to allow your body to gradually return to a normal pace after strenuous activity.

Start your general warm-up by moving around to increase the circulation of blood. Try light calisthenics or jogging along the lines of the court. For example, jog around the court twice, or combine jogging toward the net, backpedaling away from the net, and shuffling steps (one foot never crosses in front of the other) to move laterally across the court while facing the net. After you've increased your circulation, your muscles are warm and ready to be stretched. Hold each stretch for 8 seconds without bouncing and repeat each stretch at least twice. Include stretches for your upper body, back, and legs.

Now you're ready to hit. Start in the forecourt area and exchange soft, short groundstrokes with your practice partner. Next, move to the baseline and hit controlled forehands and backhands. Alternate roles with your partner to practice down-the-line groundstrokes, crosscourt groundstrokes, and volleys while your partner returns with groundstrokes.

Following the match or practice session, walk the perimeter of the doubles court for 5 minutes or until your pulse rate drops below 120 beats per minute. Then repeat your stretching exercises while your muscles are still warm.

Tennis Injuries

As with any physical activity, it is possible to get hurt playing tennis. Although tennis elbow gets most of the publicity, there are several less serious, but more common, injuries among tennis players. Blisters, sprains, strains, cramps, and shin splints, as well as tennis elbow, are examples of problems almost all players encounter sooner or later (see the following chart). In most cases tennis injuries are not emergencies, and the player who has some information can take care of them personally.

Injuries, Causes, and Treatments		
Injury	**Cause**	**Treatment**
Blisters	• Racket-hand irritation • Foot, sock, shoe irritation	• Clean area • Open area to drain • Skin Lube™ • Bandage and tape
Sprains	• Joints forced beyond normal range of motion	• Ice for 24 to 48 hours • Compress • Elevate • Rest
Strains	• Overexertion • Improper warm-up • Sudden movement • Fatigue	• Ice every 20 minutes during first day after injury • Heat before playing • Ice after playing
Cramps	• Fatigue • Overexertion • Chemical imbalance	• Stretch affected muscle • Ice • Pressure • Massage
Shin splints	• Hard surfaces • Poor conditioning • Inadequate arch support • Poor running technique • Congenital problems	• Tape or elevate arch • Proper shoes • Ice • Rest
Tennis elbow	• Forearm stress • Weak muscles • Improper hitting technique • Wrong racket • Bone fragments	• Ice • Aspirin or ibuprofen • Rest • Different racket • Arm bands

EQUIPMENT: CHOOSE YOUR WEAPONS

Three kinds of equipment are offered on the market. At the low end are cheap, poorly made products. At the upper end are overpriced items with cost exceeding quality. In the middle, you can find moderately priced, high-quality rackets, tennis balls, clothes, and shoes. Here are some suggestions to help you make the right decisions.

Rackets

Tennis rackets range in price from $15 to $400. Starter rackets usually cost between $25 and $50. Serious players spend between $75 and $300 for rackets. Once a certain price level is reached, the difference is one of personal preference, not of quality. A $300 racket is not necessarily better for you than one that costs $100. When you find the racket that is best for your budget and your style of play, stop looking. Sooner or later you have to hit the ball over the net, and the racket will be just about as good as you are.

Most of the rackets manufactured today have head sizes between 90 and 110 square inches. The larger the hitting surface, the better chance you have of making contact with the ball, so buy a bigger one if you are learning the game. Metal rackets are made of steel, titanium, magnesium, and aluminum. They are durable, but some of them vibrate on contact with the ball more than other frames. A racket that vibrates will not give the feel of hitting a solid shot, especially on shots that are hit off-center. In fact, a racket that vibrates on contact is probably not transferring your power to the ball as much as it should. Other products used to make rackets include fiberglass, high modulus graphite, and Kevlar. Rackets made of these materials are strong and light, and can be stiff or flexible. Most are made of composites—two or more of the materials mentioned. Composite rackets allow you to select one that meets your needs in terms of balance, flexibility, stability, and feel. Most beginners buy aluminum or inexpensive composite rackets.

During the past 10 years, racket weights have moved in one direction—down. When the first edition of *Tennis: Steps to Success* was written, rackets ranged in weight from 11 to 14 ounces. Now the range begins at 9 ounces. In the United States, racket weight is usually stated in ounces; elsewhere, grams are used. Table 1 shows typical weights of rackets in ounces and grams.

Unfortunately, little uniformity exists in the way rackets are presented to consumers around the world. Local differences in the designations of size, weight, and even cosmetics often make the same racket look completely different in the United States, Japan, and Germany. Even though most companies designate rackets as L (Light) or SL (Super Light), the weight of one company's L racket may be different from a competitor's.

Table 1. Racket Weights in Ounces and Grams

Ounces*	Grams	Ounces*	Grams
9.0	255.1	11.0	311.8
9.1	257.9	11.1	314.6
9.2	260.8	11.2	317.5
9.3	263.6	11.3	320.3
9.4	266.4	11.4	323.1
9.5	269.3	11.5	326.0
9.6	272.1	11.6	328.8
9.7	275.0	11.7	331.6
9.8	277.8	11.8	334.5
9.9	280.6	11.9	337.3
10.0	283.5	12.0	340.1
10.1	286.3	12.1	343.0
10.2	289.1	12.2	345.8
10.3	292.0	12.3	348.6
10.4	294.8	12.4	351.5
10.5	297.6	12.5	354.3
10.6	300.5	12.6	357.1
10.7	303.3	12.7	360.0
10.8	306.1	12.8	362.8
10.9	309.0	12.9	365.7

*1 oz. = 28.35 grams

Manufacturers now stress the distribution of the weight rather than the weight itself. Rackets are either head heavy, evenly balanced, or head light. A very light racket may provide unusual power because most of the weight is in the head. Beginning players perform better with evenly balanced rackets.

Flexibility refers to how much the racket bends from end to end when the ball is hit. Some players can feel the frame flex, or give, when contact is made. Stiff frames give a little more control than flexible ones. A flexible racket may give more power, but it takes time to adjust to the feel of the frame.

Racket grips are made with circumferences between 4-1/4 to 4-5/8 inches. Those with 4-1/2-inch grips are the most common. The racket's weight and grip size may be designated on the side of the shaft. For example, L2 indicates a light racket with a 4-1/4-inch grip, L3 means light with a 4-3/8-inch grip, and L4 describes a light racket with a grip that is 4-1/2 inches in circumference. Use these four methods to determine the right size for your hand:

■ Shake hands with the racket or hold it with an Eastern forehand grip. As your fingers curl around the grip, the end of the thumb should touch the first joint of the middle finger (see Figure 1).

■ Measure the distance from the long crease in the middle of your palm (second down from your fingers) to the tip of your ring finger. Position the ruler between your ring and middle fingers. The distance measured should be very close to the right racket circumference grip for your hand (see Figure 2).

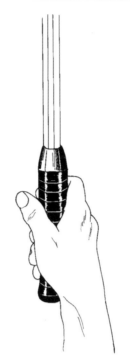

Figure 1. The end of the thumb meets the first joint on the middle finger.

- Hold the racket in your playing hand. It should feel comfortable and easy to move. The shape of the grip should fit the contour of your hand.
- Play with a demo or loaner racket. If it twists in your hand on contact, the grip may be too small. If your hand and arm tire quickly, it might be too big.

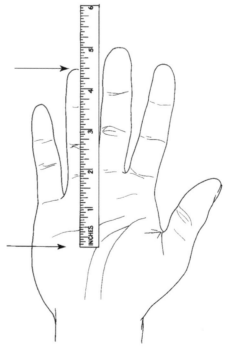

Figure 2. Measure from the tip of your ring finger to the second line in your palm.

Most players use nylon or other synthetic strings. The 2% who use gut (beef or sheep intestine) are either very good players or they are very serious about their games. Beginners should have rackets strung with 16-gauge nylon and can expect to pay $15 to $30 for a restringing job. If you play tennis twice a week, get your racket strung twice a year, even if a string does not break. If you play five times a week, have your racket strung about five times a year.

Manufacturers recommend string tensions for their rackets. Larger racket heads should be strung at higher tensions, but the general rule is to have your racket strung toward the lower end of the recommended pound range. The range is from the mid-50s to mid-70s, depending on the kind of racket. Although some players have their rackets strung as low as the 40s and as high as the 80s, don't try it.

Once you have selected the right racket and strings, take care of them. Rackets take a lot of abuse on the court during normal play. You can make them last longer and stay stronger by following these suggestions:

- Avoid storing rackets in hot, cold, or damp places.
- Keep racket covers on rackets when not being used.
- Don't spin the racket on the court to determine serve and side.
- Don't use the racket to pick up balls if the frame scrapes against the court.
- Wipe the strings clean after playing on a damp court or in high humidity.
- Use a replacement grip or overwrap when the original one becomes torn or slick.
- Don't throw your racket, bounce it off the court, or hit things with it.
- Inspect your racket for warping or breaks before getting it restrung.
- If a string breaks, remove all the strings to relieve tension on the frame.

Tennis Balls

Tennis balls come in almost as many varieties as rackets. Don't start out with cheap ones and graduate to better quality balls as you improve. Always play with good balls. Buy the best ones available the first time out. Brand names can be deceiving, but Wilson, Penn, Dunlop, and Spalding are some of the companies that make quality tennis balls.

Whatever the brand, look for information on the container that indicates the balls have been approved by the United States Tennis Association or the International Tennis Federation. Save money by watching for sales, shopping at discount stores, and buying a dozen or more balls at a time.

Most tennis balls are packaged in clear, plastic cans under pressure. If pressure has not been maintained and the balls are spongy when the can is opened, return it to the dealer for a refund or a new can. If a ball breaks within the first 2 or 3 sets, the can of balls should be returned for replacement.

You can't play with one can of balls forever. Three balls may last two or three outings for beginners and some intermediates, but after that they will begin to lose their pressure and bounce, or the fuzz will wear off. When that happens, use them for practice only. Extend the life of balls by keeping them in the original container and by storing them in a cool place.

Some tennis balls are not packaged under pressure and are sold in a box. These balls are not as bouncy as those that are pressurized, but they never go completely dead. They will eventually lose their fuzz and that will affect the bounce of the ball.

Ask for heavy-duty balls if you are going to play on hard surfaces like concrete. Regular "championship" balls are used on softer surfaces because they do not wear as quickly. Tennis balls designed for play at high altitudes are also available.

Footwear

The five factors to consider in buying tennis shoes are cost, durability, comfort, weight, and appearance. Shoes vary widely in price. Discount stores sell affordable shoes that will get you through a course or a series of lessons with no problems. If you plan to continue playing, it might be better to invest in a more expensive and more durable shoe.

How often you play, your style of play, and the court surface will determine how much wear you will get from your shoes. People who play often on hard surfaces may wear out a pair of shoes within a few weeks. Those who play on softer surfaces may get months out of their shoes. It is not unusual for the toe of one shoe to wear out completely while the rest of the shoe is still in good condition. Leather-topped shoes may be more comfortable than those with canvas, but they are also more expensive and may be heavier. If you are a player who wears out the sole or toe quickly, the comfort may not be worth the expense.

Buy the lightest shoe possible if you are satisfied with the cost, comfort, and durability. A difference of a few ounces will seem like pounds during the third set of a match.

For many people, the name and style of tennis shoes is more important than any other factor. If you are one of those people, remember that you may pay as much for the logo and the look as you do for durability and comfort.

Choosing the right kind of sock can be as important as your choice of shoes. Footwear companies have become more specialized in manufacturing socks for various sports. Socks designed specifically for tennis players are extremely thick and have extra padding for the toe and heel. One caution regarding thick, comfortable athletic socks: They can be so thick and cushioned you may have to buy shoes a half-size larger than usual.

Apparel

If you think tennis shoes reflect trends and advertising more than quality, wait until you shop for tennis apparel. The bad news is that you can spend a lot of money on shirts, shorts, skirts, warm-ups, and other active-wear clothing. The good news is that you can find moderately priced, high-quality tennis outfits at sporting goods, department, and discount stores, and at some pro and specialty shops.

Students in physical education classes usually wear shorts and shirts approved by the school or college. Although there may be dress codes and conformity, no emphasis is put on fashion. If you take lessons or compete in events, there are guidelines to follow. A few facilities still require white attire, but most allow colors. Stay away from tank tops and swim suits. Use common sense, observe what others are wearing, and ask a teacher, coach, tournament director, or pro what kind of dress is appropriate.

The more time you spend at the tennis courts, the better feel you will have for dressing comfortably and to fit the occasion. Most serious players practice in the most comfortable clothes they can find. They play matches in the best looking outfits they can afford.

STEP 1

RACKET AND COURT AWARENESS: GETTING STARTED

The first step in becoming a tennis player is getting used to the racket and the court. As soon as the racket feels like an extension of your arm rather than an awkward piece of equipment, you can make it work for you. When you are as comfortable moving around a tennis court as you are moving around your favorite room at home, you will be able to get to and hit all of the shots you need to be successful.

The purpose of this step is not to learn about all of the grips or all of the intricate footwork that advanced players exhibit. The purpose is to start getting your hands and feet ready to master those skills later. Many of the drills involve a forehand grip, but details of the various ways to hold the racket for backhand, serve, volley, and other shots will be discussed and illustrated later. With practice, you will begin to move in the quickest and most efficient ways to win points.

The activities that follow should help you learn to use a tennis racket as you would use any other tool and to defend a court as if it were your own private space. The order in which you do the drills in this step is not important (unlike the other steps). Racket handling and court movement exercises can be done before tennis lessons or away from the courts—anywhere with enough room. Unless you are in a tennis class in which the instructor requires a certain amount of lesson time for these kinds of activities, it is up to you to decide when, where, and how long to practice these preliminary skills.

Handling the Racket

Getting used to the racket establishes the feel for the distance between your hand and the face of the racket. While that distance is easy to see, beginning players frequently miss the ball completely, hit it on the frame, or make contact somewhere other than on the middle of the strings. The kinds of exercises you practice—hitting, stopping, bouncing, or even picking up tennis balls with the help of a racket—don't really matter. The fact that you have a racket in your hand and are using it rather than struggling with it shows that you are moving through the first step and getting ready for the second step. Improve your hand-eye coordination by using the racket handling drills in this section or by making up your own.

Good tennis players constantly move the racket in their hands—both hands. If they are right-handed, they use their left hand to hold the racket at the shaft (between the handle and the head) while they make slight adjustments with their dominant hand. Make a habit of automatically placing your nondominant hand on the racket between shots. Use the support of your free hand to change or to get a more comfortable and secure grip on the handle with your dominant hand.

Do little things to give you a feel for the distance between your hand and the racket face. Tap the racket face in the center of the strings with your free hand. Dribble a tennis ball with the strings when you are moving around a court. Stop balls hit in your direction with the racket face rather than catching them with your free hand. To learn the parts of a tennis racket, see Figure 1.1.

Court Awareness

Getting ready to hit is as important as hitting. When you prepare well for each shot, you are in a good tactical position on the court, are in a comfortable

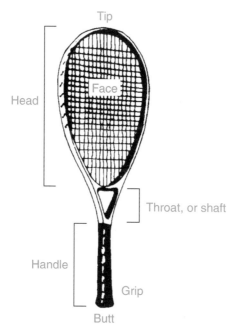

Figure 1.1 Parts of the racket.

position to hit the ball, and can choose from a variety of shot alternatives. The idea is to work hard between shots so you can relax and concentrate when it is time to hit.

Instructors will tell you things like "Be ready," "Watch the ball," and "Turn your side to the net," but those expressions can be interpreted in many ways. As you learn what the most comfortable and productive body positions are for hitting all the different strokes, figure out ways to get to those positions early. You don't have to look like every other tennis player as you move and prepare to hit; one way or another, though, you do have to physically be prepared to hit an effective shot. Listen to what your teaching pro says; then let your body put that advice into action.

Getting Ready to Hit

The ready position involves both racket handling and court awareness. It is one of the terms most frequently heard by beginners from teachers. The ready position means squaring your feet to the net, deciding how to hold your racket, bending your knees, and leaning forward (see Figure 1.2a). When you are in the ready position, you should be watching the ball leave your opponent's racket and expecting the ball to come back over the net to your side of the court every time.

Most shots are hit on the run or after you've run to get into a ready position. The latter is preferable. Run first, set up second, and hit third. Try to hit every groundstroke (shots hit after the bounce) from about the same body position. One way to get there is to shuffle laterally, sliding your feet alternately in the direction you want to go (see Figure 1.2b).

If you are really in a hurry, simply turn and run by crossing over as if you were going to pivot forward, then push off hard with the other foot. In either case, when you get to the ball, plant your back foot (the one away from the net), and step in the direction you want to hit with your other foot (see Figure 1.2c).

Where to Stand

In singles, your base of operations after the ball has been put into play should be on or just behind the baseline at the center mark (see Diagram 1.1). When in doubt, take that position and return to it after each shot. The base will change during the course of a point, depending on where your opponent hits the ball. But for now, consider the spot at the middle of the baseline as "home base."

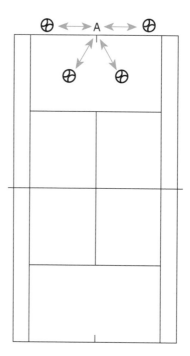

Diagram 1.1 Use the middle of the baseline as "home base" to recover between shots.

Figure 1.2

PREPARING TO HIT

READY POSITION

1. Forehand or backhand grip __
2. Racket and weight forward __
3. Opposite hand supporting racket __
4. Knees slightly bent __

SHUFFLE

1. Shuffle for close shots __

CROSS-STEP

1. Cross-step, run for farther shots __
2. Plant back foot __
3. Pivot forward __

When and Where to Move

As your opponent gets ready to hit, watch the face of his or her racket. Then focus on the ball as you move into position. If you can see the kind of spin on the ball as it approaches your side, you are doing a good job of watching the ball. You will not be able to see the ball hit your strings, but set that as a goal and track it as close to the point of contact as possible.

Knowing where to go before you hit is easy—just go to the part of the court behind and to the side of where the ball will bounce. Give the ball room to move toward your position and give yourself room to swing. Beginners frequently run right to the spot where the ball hits the court. Then they are too close to the ball to swing at it. Move quickly, but keep your swinging distance from the ball. Once you have hit the ball, return to the middle of the baseline.

RACKET AND COURT AWARENESS

DRILLS

1. Hand Dribble

Without a racket, bounce the ball with one hand 10 times, then 10 times with the other hand, and finally 20 times alternating hands with each dribble. Try to read the print on the ball or see the seams with each dribble. Let your hand move up and down with the ball to keep it going.

Success Goal = 40 total dribbles, reading the print or seeing the seams each time

    10 with one hand ___
    10 with other hand ___
    20 dribbles alternating hands ___

Success Check

• Extend your fingers ___
• Read the print or see the seams on the ball ___
• Move your hand up and down with bounce ___

To Increase Difficulty

• Stand near a line on the singles court and attempt to make each dribble hit the line.
• Increase the number of successful dribbles by 10 until you reach 100.

To Decrease Difficulty

• Practice dribbling with a large rubber playground ball or basketball before trying to dribble a tennis ball.

2. Shake Hands

Shake hands with the racket handle to learn the Eastern forehand grip. Hold the racket in your left hand (if you are right-handed) and point one edge of the racket down toward the court. Now shake hands with the racket handle. As you do, your wrist is positioned slightly to the right of the top part of the grip for right-handers (slightly to the left for left-handers). Check your partner's grip and ask him or her to check yours.

Success Goal = 10 correct handshake grips with the racket ___

✔ Success Check

- Position the racket edge down ___
- Shake hands with the racket ___
- Keep your wrist slightly to the right of the handle top (for right-handers) ___
- Hold the racket firmly ___

To Increase Difficulty

- Execute the shake hands grip with your eyes closed. Have a partner or instructor check your grip for the correct position.

3. Racket Dribble

Use an Eastern forehand grip and bounce the ball on the court, using the racket strings instead of your hand to dribble the ball. After you make contact with the ball, let your racket move up with the bounce of the ball before sending it to the court again (see Figure a).

Success Goal = 25 consecutive bounces ___

✔ Success Check

- Position the racket face and the palm of your hand down ___
- Bump the ball with your strings ___
- Let the ball rise to your racket ___

To Increase Difficulty

- Stand near a line on the court and attempt to make each dribble hit the line.
- Dribble the ball around the singles court, trying to make the ball bounce on the lines bordering the singles backcourt.
- Increase the number of successful dribbles by 10 until you reach 100.
- Practice dribbling the ball up into the air rather than down onto the court (see Figure b).
- Alternate hitting the ball up into the air with letting the ball bounce on the court.

To Decrease Difficulty

- Hold the racket with any grip that is comfortable, then gradually change to an Eastern forehand grip.

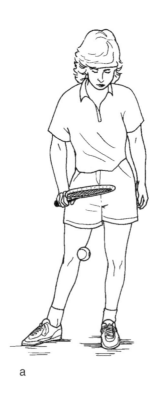

a   b

4. Ball Pickup

Try to pick up a tennis ball off the court without using your free hand. Position the ball between the inside or outside of your foot and the head of your racket. Lift up quickly with both to get the ball off the ground. Get the edge of the racket under the ball, then move your racket up and bend your knee at the same time to lift the ball. Then dribble it once or twice with your strings to get it high enough to catch with your free hand.

Success Goal = 3 consecutive balls picked up ___

Success Check
- Secure the ball between the racket and your foot ___
- Lift the ball up quickly ___
- Dribble the ball with your racket ___

To Increase Difficulty
- Lift the ball high enough to catch it before it bounces on the court.
- Lift the ball with the side of your foot you did not use on the original pickup.
- Pick up a ball off the court by getting a dribble started with the racket strings. Hold the racket like a frying pan until the ball is high enough to dribble with the shake hands grip.

To Decrease Difficulty
- Practice lifting the ball off the court without trying to pick it up with your free hand or controlling it after liftoff.

5. Ball Carry

Use the Eastern forehand grip with your palm up. Place a tennis ball on the racket strings and walk from the baseline to the net without letting the ball fall off the racket face.

Success Goal = 1 round-trip to the net and back without losing control of the ball ___

Success Check
- Use the Eastern forehand grip ___
- Position your palm up ___
- Choke up on the handle for better control ___

To Increase Difficulty
- With the ball on the racket strings, compete with a practice partner in a race from the baseline to the net and back.
- After moving from the baseline to the net and back, transfer the tennis ball from your racket face to a partner's racket without using your free hand.
- Place two balls on the strings and execute the same drill.

To Decrease Difficulty
- Choke up on the racket handle so your hand is closer to the racket head.

6. Bump Tennis

Stand about 20 feet from a partner and gently bump the ball back and forth to each other. Let it bounce in front of you as many times as necessary. Take a short backswing and let the racket do the work; hit the ball as gently as you can while bumping it toward your partner.

Success Goal = 2 minutes of bumps ___

Success Check

• Use a short backswing ___
• Hit gentle bumps ___
• Keep your free hand on the racket between bumps ___

To Increase Difficulty

• Place target tennis balls on the court 2 steps in front of you and your partner; then use the respective balls as targets as you bump a ball to each other.
• Stand a few feet from the lines that form the doubles alley; then use the lines as targets as you bump the ball to each other.

To Decrease Difficulty

• Choke up on the racket (move your hand closer to the head).

7. Toss and Catch

Without rackets, stand at the baseline facing a partner 20 feet away, 1 step behind the service line. Take turns tossing the ball to each other using an underhand motion. Take a step forward with your opposite foot when making the toss. When catching the ball, watch it moving all the way into your hands. Read the print or look for the seams with each toss. Continue for 30 throws.

This drill will help you learn how to do four things: (a) keep your eyes focused on the ball, (b) toss softly and accurately, (c) step with the opposite foot when tossing or hitting a ball, and (d) improve hand-eye coordination.

Success Goal = 30 tosses and catches without a miss ___

Success Check
- Use an underhand throwing motion ___
- Step forward with your opposite foot when you toss ___
- See the ball hit your hands when you catch ___

To Increase Difficulty
- Increase the distance between partners to 30 feet.
- Use an overhand throwing motion.
- Toss the ball so it bounces softly before it is caught.

To Decrease Difficulty
- Move closer to your practice partner by 1 step until you can successfully toss and catch the ball 30 times without a miss.

8. Grounders

Stand at the center mark facing your partner on the same side of the court. Your partner holds two tennis balls and alternately rolls them to your right and left sides. Move to the right to catch one ball, roll it back, then move to the left to catch the second ball. As you move, do not cross your feet. Learn to move with a shuffle step when you travel short distances. Keep your hips low to the ground by bending at the knees.

Success Goal = 45 seconds of play ___

Success Check
• Use a shuffle step ___
• Bend at the knees ___
• Watch the ball roll into your hands ___

To Increase Difficulty
• Increase the length of the drill by 5-second increments until you reach 1 minute.
• Have your partner roll the balls more frequently or at wider distances.

To Decrease Difficulty
• Have your partner roll the ball to where you are standing rather than from side to side.

9. Flies

Have a partner throw or hit a variety of shots from the opposite court baseline or service line. Start at the center of your baseline without a racket and move to catch balls with both hands after one bounce. Move to where the ball will come down *after* the bounce—not to where the ball first hits the court.

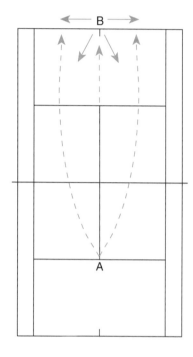

Success Goal = 10 consecutive catches ___

Success Check
• Use a shuffle step for short distances ___
• Use a cross step for longer distances ___
• Judge the location of the ball after the bounce ___
• Catch the ball with two hands ___

To Increase Difficulty
• Compete against a practice partner; the highest number of consecutive catches wins.
• Catch the balls with one hand instead of two.

To Decrease Difficulty
• Form a giant circle with your arms extended in front of your body, then move to a position where the ball can fall through the circle after the bounce (instead of trying to catch the ball).

10. Side-to-Side

Hold your racket and stand in the middle of the service court near the net. Use a shuffle step or a cross step to move past the singles sideline as fast as you can, then change directions and move toward the center service line. To change directions, plant one foot and use it to push off in the opposite direction. Keep a low center of gravity to maintain balance. Cross both lines with both feet.

Success Goal = cross each line 10 times in 30 seconds ___

Success Check
• Use a shuffle or cross step ___
• Plant your foot to change directions ___
• Stay low to maintain balance ___

To Increase Difficulty
• Compete against a partner to see how many times you cross each line during a 30-second period.
• Start on the center service line and extend the running distance by moving between the doubles sidelines.

To Decrease Difficulty
• Compete against a partner to see how many times you cross each line during a 20-second period.

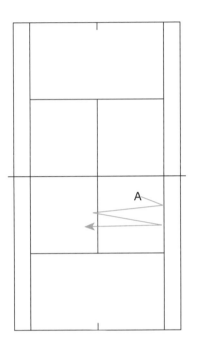

11. The Wave

Start at the center mark on the baseline. Have a partner stand 20 feet in front of you and signal you to move forward, backward, right, or left. Carry the racket in the ready position and move in the direction indicated. Use the shuffle step when moving to the side. Keep your head up and stay under control. Make your body flow smoothly in any direction. Don't jerk around the court.

Success Goal = 45 seconds without stopping ___

Success Check
• Use a shuffle step to move to the side ___
• Plant your foot to change directions ___
• Keep your racket in the ready position ___

To Increase Difficulty
• Carry a cup of water instead of a racket and try to keep the water from spilling as you move around the court.
• Increase the length of the drill by 5-second increments until you reach 1 minute.

To Decrease Difficulty
• Perform the drill for 30 seconds instead of 45 seconds.

12. Shuffle Off to Buffalo

Take a ready position behind the baseline at the center mark and use the shuffle step to move to either side, then plant one foot and pivot toward the net with the other. Shuffle back to the starting place and to your ready position, then shuffle to the opposite side.

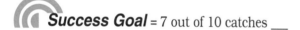 **Success Goal** = 10 repetitions to each side ___

Success Check
- Use a shuffle step to move to the side ___
- Plant one foot; pivot forward (toward the net) with the other ___
- Return to the ready position ___

To Increase Difficulty
- Have a partner stand in front of your position and indicate with hand signals the direction you are to move.
- Increase the number of repetitions by 5 until you reach 25.

To Decrease Difficulty
- Practice moving only to the right until you are comfortable with the footwork. Then practice moving only in the opposite direction.

13. String Catch

Have a partner softly toss a ball to the side of your body on which you hold the racket. Instead of hitting the ball, try to stop it with your racket strings, then catch it with your free hand before it hits the ground. Let the racket head "absorb" the ball to make a soft catch, not a hard one.

Success Goal = 7 out of 10 catches ___

Success Check
- Hold the racket firmly ___
- Let the racket head give as you stop the ball ___

To Increase Difficulty
- Bounce the ball twice on your strings before catching it with your hand.
- Bounce the ball once on your strings, let it bounce on the court, then bump it back to your partner.

To Decrease Difficulty
- Stop the ball with your racket strings without attempting to catch it with your free hand. Just let the ball fall to the court after it hits your strings.

14. Net Bump

Stand inside one of the service courts and across the net from your partner. Bump the ball back and forth as many times as you can. Don't worry about the net—the worst thing that can happen is that the ball will hit the net and you will have to start over. Slant your racket up a bit to clear the net.

Success Goal = 4 consecutive bumps (after the bounce) ___

Success Check
- Bump the ball softly ___
- Move your feet between bumps ___
- Return to the ready position ___

To Increase Difficulty
- Continue the bumps until someone misses.
- Keep score; the first player to miss 5 shots loses.
- Expand the playing area to both service courts.

To Decrease Difficulty
- Place a bench on or behind the court, use it as a net, and bump across the bench.

RACKET AND COURT AWARENESS SUCCESS SUMMARY

If you can manipulate the racket in your hand without thinking about it and easily move around a tennis court, you are on your way to becoming a good player. People who have played tennis for years cannot do what you have already learned.

Before you move to the next step, ask a partner or instructor to use the checklist in Figure 1.2 to rate your success on getting into a ready position, moving to hit, and watching the ball.

People who play tennis only during lessons, classes, or formal practice sessions do not become very good tennis players. Those who become successful and enjoy the game play and practice every time they get the opportunity. Move through your personal Steps to Success at a faster pace by putting in extra playing and practice time.

STEP

2 GROUNDSTROKES: BUILDING A FOUNDATION

Andre Agassi and Mary Pierce don't hit groundstrokes—they attack tennis balls. Watch them scorch a forehand or launch a two-handed backhand. It makes you want to hit something, too. Follow their example—learn to attack from the baseline.

A groundstroke is a shot hit after the ball bounces on the court. A forehand groundstroke comes toward the side of your body where you hold the racket. It is the most frequently hit shot in tennis and the easiest to learn. The backhand groundstroke comes toward the side of the body opposite to which you hold the racket. Although it is a natural stroke for some players, the backhand is generally considered harder to learn and a potential weakness for opponents to exploit.

Why Are Groundstrokes Important?

At least half of the shots hit in tennis are forehands. Since you will be hitting thousands of forehands, and because this shot can become a powerful weapon in your tennis arsenal, it's very important. Groundstrokes not hit with a forehand have to be hit with a backhand. If your backhand is weak, expect to see many more shots directed to that side of your body; if it's adequate, opponents won't pick on it; and if it's strong, you can use it as another way to win points.

Forehand

With one edge of the racket pointing toward the court, shake hands with the racket as if you were going to shake hands with another person. Curl your fingers around the grip near its base. As you hold the racket out to the right side (if you are right-handed), your palm should be slightly behind the handle, your wrist should be slightly to the right of the top of the handle, and the V formed by the thumb and index finger should be above but slightly toward the back part of the handle (review Figure 1, page 11). Left-handers, hold the racket so your wrist is slightly to the left of the top of the grip as you look down over the top. This is the Eastern forehand grip.

As soon as you know the ball is going to the forehand side, begin the backswing (see Figure 2.1a). The backswing is made by bringing the racket back either in a straight line parallel to the court or in a slight up-then-down loop, to a position where the racket is a bit lower than waist high and pointing to the fence or wall behind the baseline. If the racket head can be seen behind your body by a person standing across the net, it is probably too far back. Waiting to position your racket until the ball bounces does not allow you enough time to adjust to unexpected bounces, spin, or velocity. If the racket is already back when you move into position, all you have to worry about is hitting.

As the ball comes to your forehand side, move into a position so that your opposite shoulder points to the ball and your forward foot forms a line approximately parallel to the sideline (see Figure 2.1b). If you are left-handed, the right shoulder should point to the ball and your right foot will move forward parallel to the sideline. Use the foot away from the net to push off and transfer your weight forward as you begin to swing at the ball. As you hit, make sure that your weight moves forward. Some players take a small step forward with the foot closer to the net just before they hit the ball.

The forward weight transfer is one of the most important parts of any groundstroke. If it is not part of the stroke, power will only be provided by your arm instead of by the entire weight of your body. This causes weak shots and arm fatigue before the match or practice session is completed. One way to determine if your weight is on the foot closest to the net is to look at the position of your shoulder closest to the net. If that shoulder is about even with the other shoulder or is in a downward posture, your weight is forward. If the shoulder is pointing up, the weight is still on the rear foot.

Your racket should move parallel to the court or in a slightly upward trajectory during the forward swing. This upward and forward action puts a little topspin on the ball, which helps make strokes consistent and balls bounce high on the other side of the net. Make contact with the ball just before it reaches a point even with the midsection of your body. You won't be able to do that on every shot, but set it as a goal.

Keep your wrist firm and in a position that forms a curve with the top of your forearm. Do not let your wrist move during the swing. Think of sweeping something off of a table. Extend your arm comfortably, but not completely with the swing. Try to "carry" the ball on the racket strings. Hold the racket tightly enough so it does not twist on impact, but not so tightly that your feeling for the racket is lost.

After the hit, follow the ball with the racket. In this follow-through, try to reach out toward the net (see Figure 2.1c). When the racket cannot go any farther forward, cross it past the front of your body and finish high, pointing in the direction of the shot.

Every time you hit a forehand, the total action in the swing should be about the same (see Figure 2.1). If the ball comes lower than your waist, bend your knees, keep your back straight, and use the same motion. Do not stand straight up and take a golf swing at the ball. If the ball bounces deeply in the backcourt and high to your forehand, retreat quickly, plant your back foot, and move your weight forward with the swing. If a ball falls short in your court, move up, plant, step, swing, and follow through.

Figure 2.1

KEYS TO SUCCESS

PREPARING TO HIT

PREPARATION

1. Eastern forehand grip ___
2. Draw racket back early ___
3. Turn side to net ___
4. Step toward target ___

EXECUTION

1. Shift weight forward ___
2. Swing parallel to court ___
3. No wrist movement ___
4. Focus on the ball ___
5. Make contact early ___

FOLLOW-THROUGH

1. Continue swing after hit ___
2. Swing out, across, up ___
3. Point racket toward target ___

Backhand

You can hold the racket for a backhand in at least three acceptable ways. The most common grip is the Eastern backhand. With this grip, a right-hander's wrist should be slightly to the left of the top of the racket handle (looking down on the racket, with its edges perpendicular to the court); a left-hander's wrist is slightly to the right of the top. Think of your thumb as having a top, bottom, outside, and inside. The inside part of the thumb should be in contact with the back, flat part of the racket handle. You can align your thumb several ways along that part of the grip, but it is essential that the inside part be in contact with the racket. During a point, the thumb's position may change, but the part touching the grip should not (see Figures 2.2a and 2.2b).

Players with strong forearms may want to use the Continental grip. Here the wrist is directly on top of the racket handle. Your thumb has to provide more support from the rear because your wrist is not positioned behind the racket. Extend your thumb along the back of the grip so that the inside part is in contact, pushing against the racket handle during the stroke. The advantage of holding the racket this way is not having to change grips from the forehand to the backhand. The disadvantage is that some players feel uncomfortable hitting shots this way on ei-

ther side of the body because the Continental grip is halfway between conventional forehand and backhand grips (see Figures 2.3a and 2.3b).

The two-handed backhand is effective for many players. It adds power, helps control the swing, and provides better racket position to hit the ball with topspin. The disadvantages are not being able to reach as far for wide shots, not being able to maneu-

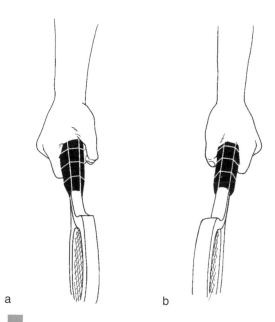

a   b

Figure 2.3 Right-handed Continental grip (a); left-handed Continental grip (b).

ver the racket easily on shots hit directly at the player, and not developing strength in the dominant arm.

For the two-handed stroke you can hold the racket two ways. The simplest is to hold an Eastern forehand with one hand and to add a forehand grip with the other (see Figures 2.4a and 2.4b). Your two hands are then touching each other, as your fingers are spread along the racket grip. Some players prefer to hold a regular backhand grip with the strong hand, then add a forehand grip with the other. Either method is okay; just find the style most comfortable for you.

Regardless of how you hold the racket, start taking it back as soon as the ball leaves the other player's racket. Use your free hand to cradle the racket at the throat or shaft (see Figure 2.5a). Leave that hand on the racket throat during the entire backhand unless you are using the two-handed stroke. As the racket goes back, rotate your shoulders far enough so that your opponent can see your back. Bring your racket back in a line parallel to the court, slightly above

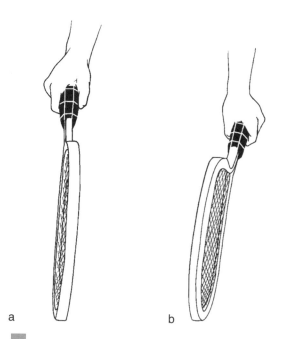

a   b

Figure 2.2 Right-handed Eastern backhand grip (a); left-handed Eastern backhand grip (b).

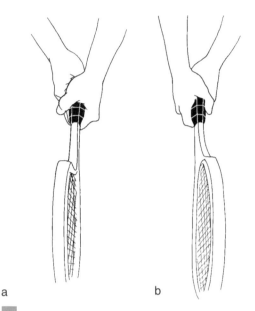

Figure 2.4 Right-handed two-hand backhand grip (a); left-handed two-hand backhand grip (b).

your waist. Think of drawing a sword out of your pocket. Learn to prepare as you move to hit. Don't wait until the last second.

Turn before contact so that your opposite shoulder is pointing in the direction of your target. Bend your knees slightly. The foot closer to the net may be pointing toward the sideline or it may be at a 45-degree angle to the net. For added power, take a small step forward with the foot closest to the net just before you make contact. Lean forward with the swing. Remember that if the shoulder closer to the net is up, your weight is on the rear foot. If it is down, though, your weight has been transferred forward.

Swing in a trajectory approximately parallel to the court. If you want topspin, start the racket head lower and swing upward; put backspin on the ball by starting with the racket a bit higher than the waist. In any case, keep your wrist firmly in place throughout the swing. The racket head should be higher than

Figure 2.5 | **KEYS TO SUCCESS**

BACKHAND

PREPARATION

1. Eastern or two-handed grip ___
2. Racket back to fence ___
3. Turn side to net ___
4. Step toward target ___

EXECUTION

1. Shift weight forward ___
2. Swing parallel to court ___
3. Focus on the ball ___
4. Make contact early ___

FOLLOW-THROUGH

1. Continue swing after hit ___
2. Swing out, across, up ___
3. Point toward target ___

your wrist on all but very low shots, unless you use a two-handed backhand. Make contact with the ball when it is even with or in front of the foot closer to the net (see Figure 2.5b). This adds power and allows you to use the pace put on the ball by the other player. Two-handers can wait longer to make contact.

Follow through out toward the net, across the front of your body, and up, in that order (see Figure 2.5c). Think of reaching out for the net with the back of your hand, then bring the racket across. Finish the stroke by pointing in the direction of the target.

Returning Groundstrokes

As soon as you hit one groundstroke, start preparing for the next one. Don't wait to see where your shots will bounce. Move to a position on or near the center of the baseline on your side of the court (review Diagram 1.1). From that position, you can usually cover all of the court on your side. If your opponent returns with a forehand, the shot is more likely to come back with pace and depth. If he or she hits a backhand, it is less likely to be hit as forcefully or as deep.

In either case, quickly position yourself so that your side is pointing to the net and your racket is moving in a backswing position waist high or slightly higher. If you are holding the racket with two hands, the racket head may be lower than your waist when the forward part of the swing begins. Anticipate where the ball will bounce, then try to get to the ball before it descends after the bounce. If you can hit balls on the rise, you can use the power of your opponent's shots to create your own power.

Think of what you are trying to accomplish with your groundstrokes and anticipate the same shots from your opponent. If groundstrokes are hit correctly, they will go high over the net, deep into the backcourt, or to an open part of the court. If all of those things happen, you can counter the groundstroke attack by getting into a position to defend your court. If those things do not happen, your opponent will have hit a weak shot, leaving an opening for a return with your killer groundstroke.

Groundstroke Combinations

Whether hitting with a friend, going through drills in a practice session, warming up, or playing a match,

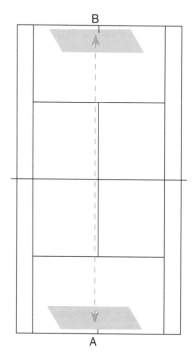

Diagram 2.1 A and B hit controlled groundstrokes from the baseline.

the one thing that tennis players do most is hit groundstrokes back and forth from the baseline (see Diagram 2.1). Although serves, volleys, lobs, smashes, and other shots are important parts of the game, nothing is more important or more basic to tennis than being able to keep the ball in play from the baseline. After you have progressed through the forehand and backhand phases of your game, the next step is to hit combinations of groundstrokes consistently enough to play points.

Once a ball has been put into play, you have to repeatedly hit shots from a variety of locations along the baseline. Here are some suggestions to help develop your baseline game:

- Change grips between forehand and backhand strokes.
- Use your free hand to adjust grips between shots.
- Return to a central position (usually the baseline center mark) between shots.
- Be patient and keep the ball in play.

GROUNDSTROKE SUCCESS STOPPERS

It is not enough to merely recognize problems executing forehands and backhands—you must also be able to make a correction to solve those problems.

Here are some common groundstroke flaws and ways to fix them.

Error	Correction
1. You are holding the racket with the wrong grip.	1. Use your free hand to adjust grips between shots. Remember that as you look at the grip from the top, your wrist should be behind and to the right of top on a forehand; behind and to the left on a backhand.
2. The racket twists in your hand when the ball hits it.	2. Hold the racket tighter.
3. You do not have enough time to hit.	3. Start preparing when the ball leaves your opponent's racket. Don't wait until it bounces on your side.
4. You are hitting shots too hard or too deep.	4. Reduce the length of your backswing. Keep the racket face perpendicular to the court.
5. You cannot hit with power.	5. Your weight should be forward when you make contact. Take an early backswing and move the racket forward through the swing. No follow-through causes a short, weak shot. Don't hit a backhand with a forehand grip.
6. Your shots are inconsistent.	6. Check your grip and keep your wrist in a fixed position. The more movement, the less control.
7. Your elbow is high and is the first part of your arm to move forward during a backhand.	7. Keep your elbow closer to your waist when you hit a backhand. Don't lead the stroke with that part of your arm.

DRILLS

1. Shadow Swings

Practice alternating the forehand and backhand swings in front of a mirror. Say to yourself, "Ready, pivot, step, swing." Develop a smooth motion as you pretend to hit. If you don't have a large enough mirror, visualize your swings as you go through the motions.

Success Goal = 50 alternating forehand and backhand swings ___

Success Check
• Stand in the ready position ___
• Turn your side and bring the racket back ___
• Step forward and swing ___

To Increase Difficulty
• Close your eyes and visualize your swing.
• Close your eyes, execute the swing, and have a partner critique it.

To Decrease Difficulty
• Go through the sequence one step at a time instead of completing all four phases (ready; then ready, pivot; then ready, pivot, step; and finally, ready, pivot, step, swing).

2. Drop-and-Hit Forehands

Stand with your nonracket shoulder towards the net. Drop a ball (don't throw it down) to your forehand side, let it bounce up, then hit it over the net with a forehand stroke. Hit the ball at a safe distance over the top of the net and try to hit it as far into the opposite backcourt as possible.

Few players put the ball in play by dropping and hitting with a backhand; it is more comfortable and practical with a forehand.

Success Goal = 10 forehand groundstrokes into the target area ___

Success Check
• Stand with your side to the net ___
• Drop the ball in front of you and to the side ___
• Aim deep ___

To Increase Difficulty
• Drop and hit to the backcourt target area.
• Drop and hit crosscourt forehands.
• Drop and hit down-the-line forehands.
• Hit each shot with topspin (use a low-to-high swinging motion).

To Decrease Difficulty
• Move to a position halfway between the baseline and the service line to put the ball into play.

3. Toss to Groundstrokes

Have a partner stand across the net without a racket at a distance of 20 feet from you. Your partner tosses balls first to your forehand and then to your backhand. Direct softly hit groundstrokes to your partner. Your partner should be able to catch or reach your shot with one hand or two.

Don't overswing. Work on control, not power. Develop control early as a tennis player. If you are good enough to hit the ball at a tosser or hitter, you will be good enough to hit away from your opponent during a match.

Success Goal = 15 consecutive forehands caught by partner ___

15 consecutive backhands caught by partner ___

✔ Success Check

• Use a compact swing ___
• Focus on the ball ___
• Swing through ___

To Increase Difficulty

• Have your partner increase the pace of tosses.
• Move to the baseline to return shots.
• Return to the center of the baseline after each shot.
• Use a shorter swing on tosses that have more speed.

To Decrease Difficulty

• Concentrate on making contact with the ball 15 consecutive times rather than trying to direct the ball to your practice partner.

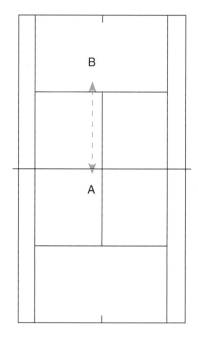

4. Wall Ball Groundstrokes

Stand 20 feet from a wall. Try to keep the ball in play against the wall with softly hit forehands or backhands. Drop and hit to put the ball into play. Again, the emphasis is on maintaining control of the ball, not trying to hit the ball hard.

Success Goal = 15 consecutive forehands off wall ___

    15 consecutive backhands off wall ___

Success Check
- Drop and hit to put ball in play ___
- Use soft groundstrokes ___
- Practice control, not power ___

To Increase Difficulty
- Increase the pace of your shots.
- Hit every shot with a forehand.
- Hit every shot with a backhand.

To Decrease Difficulty
- Move 2 steps closer to the wall.
- Set a Success Goal of 2 consecutive shots, then increase the goal by 1 until you reach 15.

5. Alternating Wall Ball Groundstrokes

Repeat Drill 4, but alternate hits against the wall with a practice partner. Hit, then use a shuffle step to get out of the way for your partner to hit. Do not turn your back to the wall. Remember: Hit and move!

Success Goal = 20 total consecutive groundstrokes between you and your partner ___

Success Check
- Use a short swing ___
- Shuffle step out of the way ___
- Hit and move ___

To Increase Difficulty
- Return every stroke with a forehand (or with a backhand).
- Increase the Success Goal by increments of 10 until you reach 50.

To Decrease Difficulty
- Practice hitting against the wall with your partner, but do not alternate shots unless the ball returns to other player.

6. Groundstroke Service Court Rally

Stand on or behind the service line; turn your side to the net, then drop the ball and softly hit a forehand to your partner on the other side. Keep the ball in play with forehands and backhands, hitting all shots so that they bounce into the opposite service court. As soon as you hit 1 shot, start preparing for the next one by using your free hand to adjust the grip and by returning to a central position behind the service line.

Resist the temptation to move inside the baseline after every shot. If you do, shots will come at your feet too often. It is easier to move forward to get to short shots than to move backward to return deep ones.

Success Goal = 20 consecutive hits between partners __

Success Check
• Position your side to the net __
• Use short hits __
• Use your free hand to adjust your grip __

To Increase Difficulty
• Move 3 steps back and continue hitting.
• Hit forehands only.
• Hit backhands only.

To Decrease Difficulty
• Conduct the drill with the instructor or an advanced player (better players can stabilize a drill by being consistent and hitting shots easy to return).

7. Service Court Groundstroke Games

Repeat Drill 6, keeping score with the no-ad system. Drop the ball to put it into play. The first player to win 4 points wins the game. Try to hit away from the other player. Don't hit hard; just try to place the ball in open areas of the court.

Success Goal = play 2 out of 3 games, 3 out of 5 games, or a complete set (when one player wins at least 6 games and leads by at least 2 games) ___

Success Check
- Bring the racket back early ___
- Hit to the open court ___
- Move your feet ___

To Increase Difficulty
- Extend the playing area to the entire singles court.
- Keep the ball in play 4 shots before either player can win the point.

To Decrease Difficulty
- Play points instead of games. This takes the pressure off thinking about more than the point being played.

8. Baseline Setups

Take a position at the baseline and have a partner put balls into play to either your forehand or backhand. Return the ball so it lands anywhere in the opposite backcourt.

Work on depth as well as technique. The key to getting the ball deep is to hit it higher over the net, not just to hit it with more power.

Success Goal = 10 forehands ___ 10 backhands ___

Success Check
- Safely clear the net with the ball ___
- Aim for your opponent's backcourt ___
- Follow through after contact ___

To Increase Difficulty
- Have your partner increase the pace of setup shots.
- Prior to the shot, call out which side of the backcourt your shot will land (left or right).

To Decrease Difficulty
- Have your practice partner feed you 2 forehands for every backhand.

9. Running Groundstrokes

Have a partner stand at the net with a basket of balls and toss or hit balls alternately to your forehand, then backhand. Count the number of consecutive shots you return into the singles court. Use your opposite hand to maneuver the racket and change grips between strokes.

Success Goal = 20 consecutive groundstrokes into the target area ___

Success Check
- Change grips between forehands and backhands ___
- Return to the ready position between shots ___

To Increase Difficulty
- Have your partner toss or hit shots randomly to either side (rather than alternating shots).
- Increase the number of consecutive groundstrokes by increments of 5 until you reach 50.

To Decrease Difficulty
- Have your partner wait until you have returned to the ready position at the center mark before tossing or hitting the next ball.

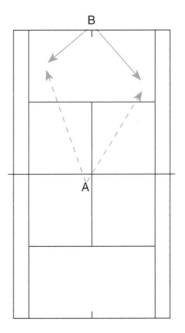

10. Water Torture

Before the drill begins, fill a paper cup with water, then position yourselves as you did in Drill 9. Have your partner stand near the net and toss or hit balls to your forehand only while you hold the cup in one hand and hit groundstrokes with the other. The objective is to maintain your balance so well that you can move and hit without spilling the water.

Success Goal = 10 consecutive groundstrokes hit into the singles court without spilling a drop of water ___

Success Check
- Glide to the ball; don't bounce ___
- Swing smoothly without jerking the racket ___

To Increase Difficulty
- Have your partner hit shots alternately to your forehand and backhand.

To Decrease Difficulty
- Conduct the drill with a half-filled cup of water.

11. Footwork Scramble

Stand in the middle of your service line. Have a partner sit down behind the net on the other side of the court with a basket of balls and toss shots anywhere inside the service court for 30 seconds. Every time you hit, another ball is immediately tossed to a different spot in the court.

Use short steps, short bursts of speed, and short strokes to get the ball back. Concentrate more on footwork than on strokes.

Success Goal = return every shot attempted for a 30-second period; missing none is a perfect score ___

Success Check
• Use short steps ___
• Plant your foot to change directions ___
• Use short swings ___

To Increase Difficulty
• Increase the time period by 10-second increments up to 1 minute.
• Return every shot with a forehand, regardless of where the ball is tossed.

To Decrease Difficulty
• Have your practice partner toss all balls to the forehand side of the service court.

12. Baseline Rally

Stand on or behind the baseline. Drop the ball to put it into play, and keep it in play by hitting into the opposite singles court. Concentrate on the ball—not your opponent, the net, or any other distraction. Return to the center of the baseline after each shot.

Success Goal =20 consecutive hits between you and your partner ___

Success Check
• Focus on the ball ___
• Readjust grip between shots ___
• Prepare early for the next shot ___

To Increase Difficulty
• Use only the right or left backcourt as a target area.
• Increase the Success Goal by increments of 10 up to 50 shots.
• Hit most of your baseline shots crosscourt.
• Shorten your backswing when you run forward to hit a shot.
• Practice hitting 5 consecutive shots to one target area, then hit shot 6 to a different area of the court.

To Decrease Difficulty
• Both players move to positions just behind the service line, hit softly, and gradually move back to the baseline area.

13. Crank It Up

Start at the baseline and have a partner feed you shots into the backcourt area. Return the first 10 shots at 50% velocity on both the forehand and backhand sides. Shots returned at half speed are more likely to land in the forecourt area (between the net and the service line). Return the next 10 shots at 75% velocity. Then return the last 10 shots hitting as hard as you can. Harder hit balls have a better chance of landing in the backcourt. Get help from your partner in judging the velocity of your shots.

Success Goal = 10 of 10 forehand and backhand returns at 50% speed ___
  6 of 10 returns at 75% speed ___
  3 of 10 returns at 100% speed ___

Success Check
• Use a firm grip ___
• Swing smoothly ___
• Shoot deep ___
• Recover quickly ___

To Increase Difficulty
• Count only those shots that land in the opponent's backcourt.
• Count only those shots that land in the opponent's backhand side of the court.
• Increase the Success Goal to 7 of 10 at 75% and 5 of 10 at 100%.
• Alternate returning shots down the line and crosscourt.

To Decrease Difficulty
• Practice only the 50% and 75% returns.

14. Down-the-Line Groundstrokes

Keep the ball in play from the baseline area, hitting only down-the-line groundstrokes to your partner. Change positions so that you practice both forehand and backhand groundstrokes.

Don't aim at the sidelines. Leave room for error so that off-target shots still have a chance to go in.

Success Goal =100 total attempts between you and your partner (50 shots per player) ___

✔ Success Check
• Backswing early ___
• Be quick on your feet ___
• Follow through toward the target ___

To Increase Difficulty
• Set Success Goals of 10, 20, 30, 40, 50 in shots rather than attempted shots.

To Decrease Difficulty
• Move forward to a position between the service line and the baseline to continue the rally, but hit with less pace to counter the reduced distance.

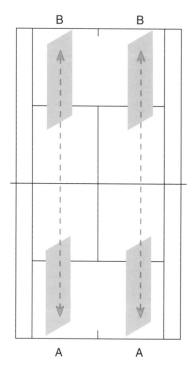

15. Figure-8 Groundstrokes

Players A and C stand at one baseline while players B and D face them from the opposite baseline. Player A drops a ball and hits it crosscourt to B. B returns with a down-the-line groundstroke to C, who directs the next shot crosscourt to player D, who hits down the line to A. The players continue hitting groundstrokes in the figure-8 pattern. Any player can begin a new cycle of shots after a miss.

Success Goal =12 consecutive groundstrokes (3 cycles of 4 shots) without an error ___

✔ Success Check
• Step in the direction of your shot ___
• Follow through in the direction of your shot ___

To Increase Difficulty
• Increase the number of successful groundstrokes by multiples of 4.

To Decrease Difficulty
• All players move forward to a position behind the service lines and execute the same pattern of strokes, hitting with less pace and depth.

16. Crosscourt Groundstrokes

Line up slightly to one side of the center mark. Keep the ball in play with your partner, hitting crosscourt shots only. Change your positions so that you practice both forehand and backhand shots. Leave a space for your practice partner to hit. Don't start so far to either side that you are standing in the corner.

Success Goal =100 total attempts between you and your partner (50 shots per player) __

Success Check
- Step in the direction of the target area __
- Strike the ball on the rise __
- Recover quickly after the shot __

To Increase Difficulty
- Try to hit every shot so that it bounces between the opposite service line and the baseline.

To Decrease Difficulty
- Move closer to the net and keep the ball in play with softly hit groundstrokes.

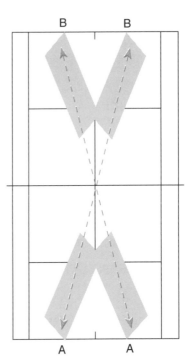

17. Consecutive Crosscourt Groundstrokes

Line up on the baseline slightly to one side of the center mark. Keep the ball in play with your partner by hitting only crosscourt shots, but count the number of consecutive shots played by both hitters without an error. With each error, start the count again. Concentrate on preparation and control, not power. Try to get into a groove so that you don't have to think about hitting.

Success Goal =100 errorless groundstroke exchanges between you and your partner __

Success Check
- Move your feet continuously between shots __
- Play the ball, not your opponent __
- Establish a hitting groove __

To Increase Difficulty
- Establish a goal of 125 consecutive groundstroke exchanges.

To Decrease Difficulty
- Conduct the drill from a midcourt position, hitting soft, short groundstrokes instead of harder, deeper shots.

18. Alleys Only

You and your practice partner stand on opposite ends of the court, behind the alley. Keep the ball in play with a combination of forehands and backhands, trying to make all shots land in your partner's alley.

Success Goal = 5 shots that bounce in the alley ___

Success Check
- Work on control, not power ___
- Aim for a general target area ___
- Move into a position to practice forehands and backhands ___

To Increase Difficulty
- Alternate hitting forehands and backhands.
- Hit 5 shots into the target area in 1 minute.

To Decrease Difficulty
- Hit softer shots from a position between the service line and the baseline.

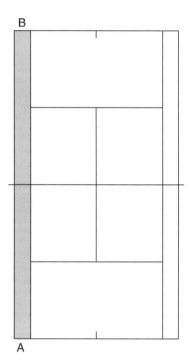

19. Two-Minute Drill

Start at the baseline. Return balls tossed to or hit to your forehand and backhand by your practice partner for a 2-minute period.

Force yourself to get to every shot, no matter how far away it is. Don't worry about how you look; worry about covering the court and doing whatever it takes to get the ball back.

Success Goal = return at least half the shots attempted during a 2-minute period ___

Success Check
- Don't watch your shots ___
- Shorten your swing when in trouble ___
- Practice a "get to everything" attitude ___

To Increase Difficulty
- Return all shots with forehands.
- Return all shots to your opponent's backhand side.
- Increase the time period by 10-second increments.

To Decrease Difficulty
- Have your practice partner feed all shots first to your forehand, then only to your backhand.

20. Groundstroke Games

From the baseline, drop a ball and put it into play against a partner. Keep it in play for at least 2 shots before trying to win the point. Every shot has to be hit with a groundstroke. The first player to win 10 points wins the game.

Look for openings on the other side of the court. Once the ball has been hit twice, hit to where your partner is not, rather than where he or she is on the court.

Success Goal = win at least half the games played ___

Success Check
- Work for good court position ___
- Hit to open spaces ___
- Hit shots deeply into your partner's court ___
- Return to the middle of the baseline between shots ___

To Increase Difficulty
- Increase the minimum number of in shots to 5 before trying to win a point.
- Practice against a stronger opponent or against an instructor.

To Decrease Difficulty
- Work with your practice partner as a teammate instead of an opponent. The "team" gets 1 point every time 10 consecutive shots are returned. See how many points you can win in a 5-minute period.

GROUNDSTROKE SUCCESS SUMMARY

Build your tennis game around groundstrokes. The player who can attack and defend from the baseline can be successful at every level of the game. At most levels, the person who can keep the ball in play four or five times during a point can win. Point-ending strokes such as volleys and smashes will come later.

Just remember, "ready, pivot, step, swing." Stand in a ready position with a forehand or backhand grip. Pivot to turn your side to the net. Step forward before or as you swing to get your weight into the shot. Swing smoothly through contact with the ball and continue your swing with a full follow-through. These four keys to success will establish a solid pattern for executing most strokes. Technique first, accuracy second, and power much later.

Before you continue, ask a practice partner or instructor to use the groundstroke Keys to Success checklists to rate your success (see Figures 2.1 and 2.5).

If the ball doesn't come to you, move your feet like crazy. Better than that, move your feet like Michael Chang. Fly to the ball, get set, and hit. In your mind, decide that no shot can get past you.

STEP
3
SERVE: FROM PUNCH TO FULL-SWING

When Pete Sampras explodes into a serve, you know something exciting is happening. He is blasting a ball at approximately 115 miles per hour at an opponent who hopes to be quick enough to react and return the shot. Let's start working on your own version of an exciting serve.

The beginner's serve is also called a punch serve or a half-swing serve. The beginning server uses it to put the ball into play at the beginning of a point. This type of serve enables you to start playing games and matches. It is not a power shot; as you get stronger and better as a tennis player, you will replace the punch with a full-swing serve.

The full-swing serve allows you to move toward the intermediate and advanced levels of the game. It is called a full-swing serve because the motion is a complete preparation to hit the ball—not just the half-swing, punch method. Instead of being only a device to get the point started, the full-swing serve becomes an important tool in your collection of strokes.

Why Is the Serve Important?

Any serve is important because a point cannot begin without one. Players alternate serving entire games throughout the match, so hitting your serve into the proper service courts is not just important—it's vital. The sooner you can master the punch serve, the sooner you can move on to a more sophisticated and effective service motion.

At the intermediate and advanced levels of the game, holding serve (winning a game when you are serving) becomes the primary objective in a match. An effective serve becomes the key to winning because it means starting 50% of the points in a match with what should be an offensive shot. If your serve

is weak, your opponent will attack it and have the chance to begin every point on the attack.

Beginner's Punch Serve

If you are a beginner, it is probably best to begin with a punch or half-swing serve. Hold the racket with an Eastern forehand (shake hands) grip. It is comfortable and allows a reasonable amount of control over the ball. As your serving motion becomes more fluid, you can change your grip to accommodate the swing.

Stand behind the baseline at about a 45-degree angle to the net, so that you are facing one of the net posts. If you are right-handed, position your left foot forward and at the 45-degree angle; if left-handed, position and angle your right foot forward. The foot away from the baseline should be placed so that if a line was drawn from the toes of that foot to the toes of the foot closer to the net, the line would point in the direction you want to serve. Put your weight on the foot away from the baseline and spread your feet wider than the width of your shoulders.

Toss the ball slightly higher than you can reach with the racket. To measure the right height of your toss, extend your arm and racket upward as high as you can comfortably reach. Now put the racket a little in front of you, so that if something were to fall off of the racket, it would fall about a foot in front of the baseline. With your arm and racket fully extended, toss the ball so it reaches a peak higher than the tip of the racket. If any toss is not where you want it to be, catch the ball or let it drop to the court. Learn to toss the ball to the right spot every time. When you do, this is one thing you don't have to worry about going wrong.

Tossing or lifting the ball for the serve also involves technique and placement. Hold the ball at the base of your fingers. Extend your arm holding the ball in the direction you want to hit and lift it without bending very much at the elbow. As you lift, release the ball at about head height by opening your fingers. The ball should go up with little or no spin.

Hold your racket with the forehand grip, stand at an angle to the baseline, and now "scratch your back" with the racket by touching the middle of your back with the edge of your racket. Lift the racket head a few inches and from this starting point, swing up at the ball you have tossed. The serving motion goes up at first rather than forward. Don't let your elbow lead the stroke; keep it high until after the hit. When you hit, reach as high as you can. Your arm and racket should be fully extended when contact is made.

As you hit, move your racket up and forward. After contact, continue to bring the racket forward (toward the net) as far as it will go. Follow through across the front of your body, ending low on the opposite side from which the motion began (see Figure 3.1).

Figure 3.1

KEYS TO SUCCESS

PUNCH SERVE

PREPARATION

1. Eastern forehand grip ___
2. Stand facing net post ___
3. Tossing arm extended forward ___
4. Racket behind head ___
5. Elbow at shoulder level ___

EXECUTION

1. Toss upward and forward ___
2. Lean forward ___
3. Reach high to hit ___

FOLLOW-THROUGH

1. Continue swing after hit ___
2. Swing out, across, down ___

Full-Swing (Intermediate and Advanced) Serve

Once you have mastered the punch serve, you are ready for a full-swing serve. Some players can skip the punch serve altogether and begin with a full-swing motion. Try it and see. If you are reasonably comfortable and successful, start with a full-swing motion.

Players with advanced serves usually hold the racket with a Continental grip. With it, the wrist is directly over the top of the racket handle as you look down on it (review Figure 2.3). Some players move their wrists a little toward the backhand side. These grips enable players to serve with control, pace, and spin. The beginner's Eastern forehand grip for the serve is mainly for control, although a few advanced players use it with a full-swing motion.

The position of your feet should be similar to that described for the beginner's serve. Your side should be partially turned toward the net so you can twist into the ball with your swing. The angle at which you stand may vary a few degrees in either direction, depending on individual preferences.

Begin with your racket out in front of your body, pointing toward the target, about chest high, and with your free hand holding the ball against the racket strings. Begin to drop your racket head in a pendulum motion, going by the side of your leg. Move the ball hand slightly downward before the toss, moving down at the same time as the racket. Move the racket arm down, then up into the back-scratching position while moving the other arm up to lift the ball for the toss. The serving motion should have a rhythmic feel.

Time the toss so that the ball will reach a point above your head and slightly in front of your body at the same time you extend your racket arm to make contact. If the timing is not right, stop everything and start over. The toss has to be far enough in front of you to force you to lean forward and beyond the baseline as you hit. Keep your head up and look at the ball while you are tossing.

As you bring the racket up and behind your back, your arm should begin to bend at the elbow and move through the back-scratching position. Fully extend your arm to make contact with the ball. When you serve, your body should be almost in a straight line

from your toes to your racket hand at the moment of impact.

To make the most of the weight transfer, move one foot during the motion. As you lean forward, keep the foot closest to the baseline in the same place, but move your other foot forward. Some players prefer to take one step, starting with the rear foot several inches behind the baseline and finishing one step inside the line.

Other players make a two-step approach with the rear foot. Bring your back foot forward to a point just behind the front foot prior to hitting. This movement results in a springboard effect on the service motion and may even give added height and leverage if you get up on your toes to hit. After you hit the ball, continue to move your foot forward, touching down 1 step inside the baseline. Regardless of the method you use, try to keep your knees slightly bent during the first part of the motion. As you hit, extend your knees to add to the springboard effect, giving your serve more power.

Follow through just like the beginners do—out toward the net, crossing in front of, and finishing down on the opposite side of your body. Figure 3.2 illustrates the complete motion for the full-swing serve.

Returning the Serve

If your opponent is serving from the right side of the court (also known as the deuce court), stand on the right of your side of the court (as you face the net) on or slightly behind the baseline, near the singles sideline (see Diagram 3.1a). When your opponent serves from the left side (the ad court), stand along the baseline on your court's left side near the opposite singles sideline (see Diagram 3.1b). If the second serve is hit with less pace, move forward 1 or 2 steps.

The beginner's serve will not be hit hard, so return it just as you would return any other groundstroke. Watch your opponent's racket face as he or she hits the serve. As soon as you determine whether the ball is coming to your forehand or backhand, adjust grips. If you are already holding a forehand grip, and the serve comes to the forehand side, no adjustment is necessary. If the serve comes to

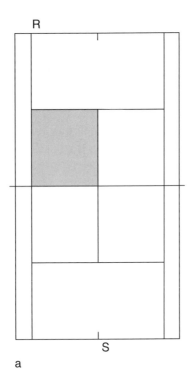

a

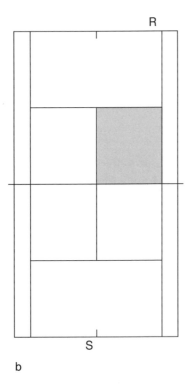

b

■ **Diagram 3.1** Receiving position when the server is serving from the right side (a), or from the left side (b).

the other side, change to either the Eastern or two-handed backhand grip.

Move to the ball while swinging your racket back toward the fence or wall behind your baseline. Then turn your side to the net, step forward, and swing in a parallel-to-the-court or slightly upward motion.

Play the ball, not your opponent. Concentrate on the service return as if you were returning forehands or backhands in a groundstroke drill. The idea is to keep the ball in play and to begin getting into a position to win the point.

Returning a full-swing serve presents a new combination of problems—the shot comes faster than a groundstroke or a beginner's serve, leaving less time to prepare to hit it back.

It is important to be extra alert to return a hard-hit serve. Get into the ready position, standing on your toes, and leaning forward. Many players take a short hop or jump just as their opponent strikes the ball. This little jump puts their bodies into motion for a quick reaction.

Most important of all, shorten your backswing. You often don't have enough time to take a full, looping swing like many players use to return groundstrokes. At the same time you take a short backswing, step forward quickly with the opposite foot. The forward step allows you to transfer your weight into the shot even though the ball is coming at you faster than usual.

Finally, do not fight power with power. If your opponent serves hard, hold your racket tightly and block the shot with your racket. Use the pace provided by the serve. If the ball comes at a slower pace, then you can go back to your normal preparation and supply the power yourself.

Figure 3.2

KEYS TO SUCCESS

FULL-SWING SERVE

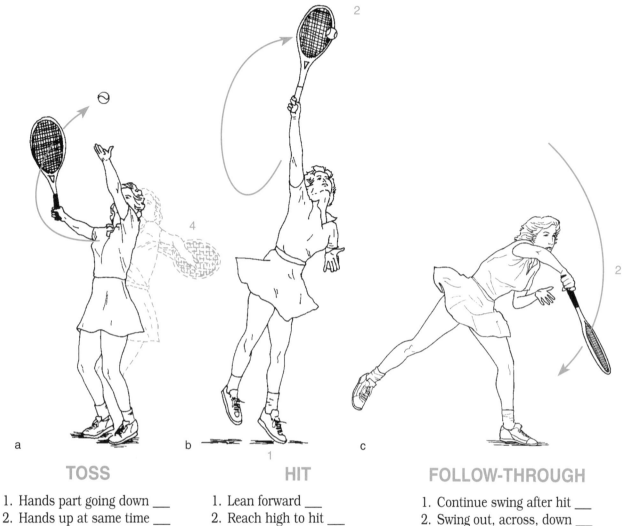

TOSS

a

1. Hands part going down __
2. Hands up at same time __
3. Lift ball upward, forward __
4. Back-scratch position __

HIT

b

1. Lean forward __
2. Reach high to hit __

FOLLOW-THROUGH

c

1. Continue swing after hit __
2. Swing out, across, down __

SERVE SUCCESS STOPPERS

The punch serve is simple and only one step in the direction of a more advanced serve. Do not expect too much from it. Problems are easy for you to recognize and relatively easy to solve. The trouble will begin when you move from the security of this serve to a complicated, but more effective full-swing serve.

Error	Correction
1. You are using a Western grip (like picking up a frying pan).	1. Use the Eastern forehand grip for the punch serve, even if it seems uncomfortable. When you are ready to try the full-swing serve, gradually change to the Continental grip.
2. Your shots lack power.	2. Don't expect any power from the punch serve. This motion provides accuracy, not power. If the ball consistently falls short on your side of the court, aim for the opposite baseline. Overcompensate. Develop two medium-paced full-swing serves instead of one bullet and one floater. Accuracy is more important than speed.
3. Your serves keep going into the net.	3. Toss the ball slightly higher than you can reach, then reach high to hit it; if you let the ball drop, the racket face will turn down and force the ball into the net.
4. Your serves go wide right or wide left.	4. With a punch serve, hold the racket with a forehand grip. The strings should direct the ball into the target area. Stand at a 45-degree angle to the baseline; a line drawn from the toes of one foot to the other should point in the direction of the service court. With a full-swing serve and a Continental grip, rotate the wrist outward (pronate) on contact to position the strings correctly.
5. Your shots are inconsistent.	5. Get a mental picture of how you and your racket should be positioned at the time of contact. Be deliberate in your approach to the serve; don't just walk up and take an unplanned swing at the ball.
6. Your serves go too deep.	6. Check the grip. If you are using a full-swing, you may have slipped back to a forehand grip. Stay with the Continental. With either serving motion, you might just be swinging too hard. Slow down.
7. You cannot get to your opponent's serves.	7. Move either right or left along the baseline before the serve.
8. You don't have enough time to prepare for service returns.	8. Stand 1 or 2 steps deeper (behind the baseline) before the serve. Take a shorter backswing.

SERVING

DRILLS

1. Ready, Aim, Throw

Throw a tennis ball from the baseline into the proper service court. Use an overhand motion similar to the one used in baseball. People who feel comfortable throwing a baseball learn to serve a tennis ball easily.

Success Goal = 20 consecutive throws into the proper court ___

Success Check
- Turn your opposite shoulder and opposite hip to the net ___
- Rotate your shoulders and hips toward the net ___
- Step in the direction of the toss with your opposite foot ___
- Move your arm down and back, bend, move forward, and extend upward ___
- Reach high before releasing the ball ___
- Follow through out, across, and down ___

To Increase Difficulty
- Change positions along the baseline before each throw.
- Throw 10 balls to the proper courts from the right side; then 10 from the left side.

To Decrease Difficulty
- Move to a position halfway between the baseline and the service line.

2. Service Toss

Take a position behind the baseline and practice the service toss. Extend your fingers as you lift the ball, imparting as little spin as possible. Try to see the ball's seams during the toss. Let the ball drop to the court. The ball should land a few inches in front of the baseline in the direction of the opposite service court.

Success Goal = 10 good tosses out of 20 attempts ___

Success Check
- Relax ___
- Execute most of the movement from your shoulder joint ___
- Extend your fingers as you toss ___
- Follow the ball with your hand and your eyes ___

To Increase Difficulty
- Toss, then catch the ball with your tossing hand.
- Place a racket cover a few inches in front of the baseline as a target for balls that have been tossed.

To Decrease Difficulty
- Line up your tossing arm with the net post or a fence post. Then follow the line of the post vertically as your arm moves upward in a tossing motion.

3. Service Line Serve

Practice serving into the proper court from the service line instead of the baseline. Alternate serving into the right and left courts. Bump the ball softly.

Success Goal = 7 accurate serves out of 10 attempts to both courts ___

Success Check
- Start with the racket behind your back or head ___
- Toss higher than you can reach ___
- Reach high to hit ___
- Keep your head and eyes up until contact is made ___

To Increase Difficulty
- Move to a position halfway between the service line and the baseline.
- Move to a position immediately behind the baseline at the center mark.

To Decrease Difficulty
- Move to a position halfway between the net and the service line.

4. Segmented Serves

Practice these parts of the service motion one at a time: (a) down (with the arm and the racket); (b) down, back (behind your back); (c) down, back, bend (your elbow); (d) down, back, bend, reach (high with the racket); and (e) down, back, bend, reach, follow through (out, across, down).

Success Goal = 25 full-swing service motions for 5 consecutive days ___

Success Check
- Start moving your tossing hand and racket hand down together ___
- Bend your arm at the elbow behind your back ___
- Fully extend your body to reach high ___
- Continue the swing after contact ___

To Increase Difficulty
- Combine the down, back, and bend phases of the motion.
- Combine the reach and follow-through phases of the motion.

To Decrease Difficulty
- Practice the segments of the swing facing a partner or instructor, who also executes the swing (follow the leader).

5. Long-Distance Serve

Practice serving into the proper courts from a position 10 feet behind the baseline. Serving from the extra distance should make you stronger and your serves more accurate once you move back up to the baseline.

Success Goal = 3 good serves out of 10 attempts to both courts ___

Success Check
• Don't be afraid to hit too hard or too far ___
• Fully extend your arm on contact ___
• Toss and lean forward ___

To Increase Difficulty
• Change from an Eastern forehand to a Continental grip.
• Move to a position 15 feet from the baseline.

To Decrease Difficulty
• Move closer to the baseline.

6. Target Serves

Place a cardboard box or similar target deep and in the middle of the service court. Look at the target before you start your motion. Hit the ball while it is high; don't let it drop. If you make a mistake, make it deep, not short.

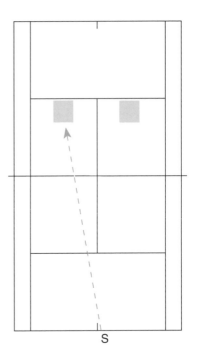

Success Goal = 2 hits out of 10 attempts ___

Success Check
- Keep your head up ___
- Shift your weight forward as you swing ___
- Land with your right foot (if you are right-handed) inside the court after the serve ___

To Increase Difficulty
- Place the targets in specific areas of the service court (backhand corner, for example).
- Set up smaller targets (a racket cover instead of a box, for example).

To Decrease Difficulty
- Set up larger targets.
- Move to a position in front of the baseline.

7. Half-the-Space Serves

Place a piece of tape across the service box (side-to-side) so the tape divides the service court into two halves. Practice the serve by aiming for the deepest area of the service court (between the tape and the service line). Think deep: If you make a mistake, the shot should go long, not short.

Success Goal = 4 serves into the restricted target area in 10 attempts ___

Success Check
- Reach high to hit ___
- Aim deep ___

To Increase Difficulty
- Move the tape closer to the service line (halfway between the service line and the location of the tape as it was previously positioned).

To Decrease Difficulty
- Move the tape closer to the net (halfway between the net and the location of the tape as it was previously positioned).

8. Read and Return

A server stands directly behind the baseline at the center mark. You and a partner wait to receive the serve on the right and left sides, respectively, of the opposite baseline. The server hits into either of your service courts without warning. "Read" clues to anticipate to which side the serve is directed, and return the serve. Start again after the serve has been returned.

**Success Goal** = 8 of 10 correct reads ___

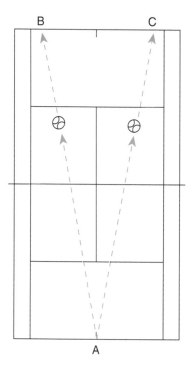

✔ **Success Check**
- Watch the server's eyes before the serve ___
- Focus on the toss for service clues ___
- Watch the angle of the racket face before impact ___
- Take a short backswing and step forward on the return ___

To Increase Difficulty
- Allow the server to serve from a position between the baseline and the service line.
- The receivers take the ready position. If one receiver thinks the serve is going to the other receiver, he or she lifts the racket above head level as the serve is delivered.

To Decrease Difficulty
- Allow the server to serve from a position 2 steps behind the baseline.

9. Serve and Return Games

Play a game with a partner using only the serve and the service return. Every serve into the proper court counts as 1 point, and every return counts as 1 point. The server gets two chances to get the ball into play. The first player to score 10 points wins. Switch server and returner roles after each game. Concentrate on your serve, not on your opponent's return.

If you are receiving the serve, stand on the baseline, just inside the singles sideline. Take a short backswing, step forward and return the ball to the backcourt of the server.

Success Goal = win at least half the games played ___

✔ **Success Check**
- Concentrate on your serve, not on your opponent's return ___
- Strive for consistency, not power ___
- Return slow, weak serves with normal groundstrokes ___
- Shorten your backswing to return faster serves ___

To Increase Difficulty
- Subtract a point for every "out" serve.
- Allow the server only one chance per point to get the ball into play.

To Decrease Difficulty
- Count 2 points for every "in" serve.

10. No-Ad Games

Now that you can hit groundstrokes and serves, it's time to play tennis. Try to win 2 out of 3 games, 3 out of 5 games, or 1 set using no-ad scoring. Remember, the first player to win 4 points wins the game. Also, if the score is 3-3 in a game, the receiver has the option of receiving the serve from either the left or right side. Do the best you can if you have to hit volleys (before the ball bounces). That step is coming later.

⌒ Success Goal = play 2 out of 3 or 3 out of 5 games ___

✔ Success Check
• Call out the score before every point ___
• Scoring is 1-2-3-game ___

▟ To Increase Difficulty
• Play 1 set or 2 out of 3 sets, starting with the score at 4-4 in each set. With the score starting at 4-4, every point is crucial. Learn to play under pressure.

11. Sets

Play a set using conventional scoring. Remember to spin a racket to determine serve and side, and to change ends of the court every time the total number of games played is an odd number.

⌒ Success Goal = play a set ___

✔ Success Check
• Call out the score before each point ___
• Use a 90-second period on changeovers to rest and regroup ___

▟ To Increase Difficulty
• Play a set in which every game starts with the score at deuce.

SERVE SUCCESS SUMMARY

The beginner's serve (punch serve) is one step through which many players advance very quickly. Keep it simple: racket back, toss high and in front, and reach high to hit. Some players are able to skip this step altogether and begin practicing the full-swing serve: arms go down together, then up together. Reach high to hit—just like Pete Sampras serving at the U.S. Open. Then follow through out, across, and down.

Whether you are using the punch serve or the full-swing serve, have your practice partner or instructor check your Keys to Success fundamentals illustrated in either Figure 3.1 or 3.2. Block everything from your mind except the task of serving. Eliminate variables. Become so mechanically efficient that you don't have to worry about fundamentals—put your body on "cruise control" to automatically execute successful serves.

SCORING QUIZ

1. In no-ad scoring, how many points do you need to win a game?

2. In no-ad scoring, on which side does the server stand when the score is 3-2?

3. In no-ad scoring, on which side does the receiver stand when the score is 3-3?

4. In conventional scoring, what is the score if the server wins the first 2 points?

5. In conventional scoring, is the server or the receiver leading when the score is 30-40?

6. In conventional scoring, what is the score if the receiver wins the first 3 points?

7. In conventional scoring, what is the score if the server wins the first 3 points?

8. In conventional scoring, what is the score if the server wins the next point after each player has won 3 points?

9. In conventional scoring, what is the score if the server loses the point when the score was 40-30?

10. What does ad in mean?

11. What does ad out mean?

12. What is the fewest number of points possible in a game?

13. What is the fewest number of games possible in a set?

14. In a pro set, how many games must be won to win the set?

15. What is the least number of points that must be won to win a tiebreaker?

16. Who serves first in a tiebreaker?

17. Where does the server stand on the first point of a tiebreaker?

18. From which sides, in order, are the second and third points of a tiebreaker served?

19. When do players change ends of the court during a tiebreaker?

20. Do players change ends of the court immediately after a tiebreaker, before the next set begins?

ANSWERS TO SCORING QUIZ

1. 4

2. Left, facing the net

3. The receiver has the option

4. 30-0

5. The receiver

6. 0-40

7. 40-0

8. Ad in (advantage server)

9. Deuce

10. The server has the advantage; if he (she) wins the next point, the game is over

11. The receiver has the advantage; if he (she) wins the next point, the game is over

12. 4

13. 6

14. 8

15. 7

16. The player who would have served the next game

17. The right side, facing the net

18. Left side, then right side

19. After every 6 points that have been played

20. Yes

STEP 4

VOLLEY: TAKING CHARGE

Boris Becker loves to get to the net and finish a point with a slicing volley. To do that, he has to be aggressive and quick. If you like action, move into Becker territory and get ready to volley.

The volley is a shot hit before the ball bounces on your side of the court. Although it is usually hit in the forecourt area, it might be used anywhere on the court. Mastering a volley requires few fundamentals, but players have little time to prepare and execute the shot. By taking a position close to the net rather than at the baseline, things simply happen faster. The only difference between a beginner's volley and that of an advanced player is the grip.

Why Is the Volley Important?

Two circumstances lead to being in a position to hit a volley. The first is when you have moved toward the net to return a shot and have no choice about the next shot. The second is when you are playing aggressively and want to end a point by putting the ball out of your opponent's reach from an attacking position near the net. In either case, the technique of hitting the shot is different from that of ground-strokes.

For advanced players, the volley becomes more than just a shot hit before the ball bounces on your side of the court. It's an important part of an offensive and defensive game plan. The position on the court from which volleys are hit and the playing level of your opponent require that the pace and location of your shots be more exact. A quick and solid stroke tells your opponent and anyone watching that they are dealing with someone who can play the entire court.

The volley is even more important in doubles, where most of the points are won and lost at the net. In singles and doubles, though, a good volley can help you improve your position on the court and move in for a winning shot. As a defensive stroke, it can keep you out of trouble and in the point until you get an opportunity to go on the attack again.

Beginner's Volley

Unlike hitting groundstrokes, hitting volleys correctly is not a very natural motion. Because you are close to the net, there is no time for much of a backswing. For the time being, use a forehand grip for forehand shots and a backhand grip for backhand shots. This will change later. The swing is more of a block or a punch, and the pace on the ball comes from your body's movement forward as much as it does from the power provided by your arm.

Stand in the ready position 8 to 10 feet from the net. Move in even closer if you are hitting volleys for the first time. Keep the racket directly in front of your body, with your arms extended. You should have the racket in a position exactly halfway between your forehand and backhand sides. Your weight should be forward so your heels are barely touching the court, if in contact at all. Bend your knees enough to get the feeling of hitting from a crouch. Bend slightly forward at the waist. As the ball approaches, you want to be in a position to spring forward to hit.

If the ball comes to your right side, use your right foot to pivot, and step forward in the direction you want to hit with your left foot (see Figure 4.1). Concentrate on moving forward instead of moving laterally along the net or pivoting in reverse.

If the ball comes to your left side, pivot on the left foot, and step across and into the ball with the right foot (see Figure 4.2). If the ball comes directly at you, slide to one side of the path of the ball by pushing off with one foot and stepping at an angle toward the net with the other.

The backswing on either side should be a short, restricted motion. As you see the ball coming, bring your racket back to a point not much farther than an imaginary line even with your back and parallel to the net. If an observer were to stand on the side opposite of your racket hand, your racket should not be visible on your backswing.

Throughout the entire motion, keep your wrist locked so that the racket forms a nearly 90-degree angle with your forearm. Lead the stroke with the racket head. Swing forward from your shoulder, not your wrist or elbow. Make contact well in front of your body. Try to hit the ball while it is rising. Attack it before it has reached you or gone behind you.

If you have stepped forward, your weight should be on the foot closer to the net. The shoulder closer to the net should be down. Direct your volleys deep into the backcourt or at an angle to pull the other player off the court.

Remember, keep your racket out in front while waiting, your weight forward, use a short backswing, and hit the ball before it reaches you. Follow through in the direction you want to hit, but recover quickly for the next shot.

To be extra alert, many players crouch low and bounce on the balls of their feet when they expect a shot to be hit right at them. If the shot comes low, do not stand straight up and put the racket down to hit the ball; bend your knees even more and get down to eye level with the ball. The angle of the racket on a low volley will be the same as on any other volley because you are bending at your knees instead of bending at your waist. Avoid volleying up on the ball (hitting it up into the air). If you volley up, your opponent will be in a position to hit down for a possible winner on the return.

Figure 4.1

KEYS TO SUCCESS

BEGINNER'S FOREHAND VOLLEY

PREPARATION

1. Eastern or Continental forehand grip __
2. Knees bent __
3. Lean forward __
4. Short backswing __
5. Turn side to net __

EXECUTION

1. Tight grip __
2. Eyes level with ball __
3. Forward with opposite foot __
4. Reach forward to hit __
5. Make contact at side __

FOLLOW-THROUGH

1. Shorter swing after hit __
2. Recover for next shot __

**Figure
4.2**   **KEYS TO SUCCESS**

BEGINNER'S BACKHAND VOLLEY

PREPARATION

1. Eastern backhand grip __
2. Knees bent __
3. Lean forward __
4. Short backswing __
5. Turn side to net __

EXECUTION

1. Forward with opposite foot __
2. Reach forward to hit __
3. Make contact at side __
4. Tight grip at contact __
5. Eyes level with ball __

FOLLOW-THROUGH

1. Shorter swing after hit __
2. Recover for next shot __

Advanced Volley

The main difference between this shot and the beginner's volley is that most intermediate and advanced players use the Continental grip. Hit all shots with the same grip—no changing from forehand to backhand—you don't have time when you are at the net against good players.

Everything else about the shot is the same as with the beginner's volley. Imagine that a rope is tied between the net and the top of your racket frame, allowing you to draw the racket back just enough to punch the ball forcefully. Now you will use the volley more frequently and with less preparation because at this level you are more often in a position near the net to use it.

Returning Volleys

In most cases, you will return your opponent's volleys with groundstrokes from the baseline area. Just as a player hitting volleys has less time to react to your shots, you have less time to return your opponent's volleys.

The first rule is not to panic. There is no need to hit harder or to try to win the point on the first shot after your opponent has moved to the net. Just put the ball where it will be difficult for the volleyer to return. This leaves you with three choices—a passing shot to the forehand side; a passing shot to the backhand side; or a lob over your opponent's head. If you can control the ball well enough to return it directly at your opponent, you're good enough to hit it away from him or her.

The second rule is to expect your groundstrokes to be returned quickly. Move your feet into position and get your racket back sooner than you would during baseline groundstroke exchanges. You may have to shorten your backswing if the ball is returned deep into your backcourt and with more pace than usual. Don't be surprised at quick returns; expect them.

VOLLEY SUCCESS STOPPERS

Some players who move into a volleying position are intimidated by opponents who hit hard, and others are discouraged from going to the net if they miss a few shots. Knowing the most common volley errors and some suggestions for correcting those errors may make you feel better about hitting volleys.

Spotting flaws in the advanced player's volley is difficult because everything is happening very fast.

It is easy just to look at the big picture and to miss a small technical error in the stroke. Most problems for players moving to the intermediate and advanced levels of tennis revolve around using the proper grip and developing reflexes to move forward into the shot.

Error	Correction
1. Your volleys lack power.	1. Step forward to move your body's weight into the shot. Check your grip. If you are trying to hit a backhand volley with a forehand grip, the back of the racket handle has no support.
2. You are making contact late.	2. Take a short backswing. Otherwise, while you are winding up, the ball will go past you.
3. The racket turns in your hand at impact.	3. Hold the racket tighter than on groundstrokes; the ball gets to you sooner and with more pace than at the baseline.
4. Your volleys hit the net.	4. Play close to the net until your skills improve. Keep your eyes at ball level and your wrist in a cocked position. Do not try to hit down on the ball; just make contact and bump it up or straight back. Open the racket face to the sky slightly, and hit "through" the ball.
5. Balls hit your strings off-center.	5. Watch the ball move into your strings. You may be looking out at where you want the ball to go instead of keeping your eyes on it.
6. Your opponent hits shots past you.	6. Be selective about going to the net. Go when your opponent has to return a deep or wide groundstroke.

VOLLEY

DRILLS

1. Shadow Volleys

Watch yourself swing through forehand and backhand volleys in a mirror. Remember to look for one component of the swing at a time (footwork, grip, or swinging motion, for example). If you can't get to a mirror, visualize yourself hitting volleys.

Success Goal = 25 forehand and 25 backhand volley swings ___

Success Check
• Use a short backswing ___
• Keep your racket head up ___
• Step forward with your opposite foot ___

To Increase Difficulty
• Close your eyes and visualize your swing.
• Close your eyes; execute the swing and have a partner critique it.

To Decrease Difficulty
• Go through the sequence one step at a time rather than completing the volley motion (footwork, grip, or racket movement, for example).

2. Baseball Glove Volleys

Have a partner toss balls to your forehand side from a distance of approximately 10 feet. Instead of hitting the balls with a racket or catching them with your bare hand, use a baseball glove to catch the balls. The motion used to catch is similar to the one used in blocking or bumping the ball in a beginner's volley. Because a tennis ball is lighter than a baseball, it might pop out of your mitt: Open the glove wide and close it tight after the catch.

Success Goal = 10 catches without a miss ___

Success Check
• Start with your hand and glove in front of your body ___
• Move the glove up and forward to make the catch ___

To Increase Difficulty
• Have your partner toss a baseball instead of a tennis ball.
• Increase the distance between you and the tosser to 15 feet.

To Decrease Difficulty
• Use a first baseman's mitt instead of a fielder's glove.
• Have your partner stand closer and toss softly.

3. Racket Catch

Have a partner stand about 20 feet from you and toss balls to both your forehand and backhand sides. Instead of hitting volleys, simply stop the ball with your racket strings as if to catch it, before it bounces.

You have worked on this type of drill in Step 2, but there you were catching the ball after the bounce. Notice how much of the work the racket and strings do by themselves.

Success Goal = 20 consecutive string catches ___

Success Check
• Watch the ball hit your strings ___
• Hold the racket tightly ___

To Increase Difficulty
• Increase the distance from your practice partner.
• Have your practice partner drop and hit balls rather than toss them.

To Decrease Difficulty
• Decrease the distance from your practice partner.
• Choke up on the racket handle.

4. Toss to Volley

Have a partner stand about 20 feet from you on the other side of the net and toss balls first to your forehand side, then to your backhand. Hit volleys anywhere in the singles court on the opposite side of the net.

Don't wait for the ball to come to you. Go forward by taking a step with your opposite foot to get to the ball.

Success Goal = 10 volleys out of 15 tosses, to each side ___

✔ Success Check
- Open your racket face (tilt it upward) slightly ___
- Don't swing; block the ball ___

To Increase Difficulty
- Return tosses with volleys that are in reach of your practice partner.
- From a baseline position, have your partner drop and hit balls instead of tossing them.
- Have your partner toss balls randomly to your forehand and backhand sides.

To Decrease Difficulty
- Decrease the distance between you and your partner.
- Choke up on the racket handle.
- Block the ball without taking a step forward with the opposite foot.

5. Back-to-the-Wall Volleys

Stand with your back against a fence or wall and return volleys tossed by a partner. Volley without your racket touching the fence or wall on the backswing; get into the habit of moving forward to hit volleys.

Success Goal = 20 consecutive volleys without touching the wall or fence ___

✔ Success Check

• Use a short, quick backswing ___
• Step forward and away from the fence ___

To Increase Difficulty

• Volley so that your partner can catch the ball without moving.
• Increase the distance from your partner.
• Have your partner increase the speed of the tosses.

To Decrease Difficulty

• Decrease the distance from your partner.
• Have your partner toss only to your forehand or only to your backhand.

6. Consecutive Volleys

Keep the ball in play hitting only volleys with a partner, who hits groundstrokes from the baseline. This is a difficult drill for beginners, but you should start getting used to the rapid exchanges. It will work better if your partner is an intermediate or advanced player. If your practice partner is at the baseline, work on getting your volleys deep into the backcourt.

Don't try to win points yet; just get used to the idea that not only can you play at the net, you can also place the ball where you want it to go. Later, you can begin hitting volleys with pace, depth, and purpose.

Success Goal = 20 consecutive volleys hit into the opposite singles court ___

Success Check
• Watch your partner's racket face at impact ___
• Hold your racket tightly ___
• Recover quickly after each shot ___

To Increase Difficulty
• Volley against two players on the baseline, alternating volleys to each.
• Have the baseline player move inside the service line to return consecutive volleys.

To Decrease Difficulty
• Have your partner move into a position just behind the service line and keep the ball in play with soft groundstrokes.

7. Two-on-One Volleys

Volley against two partners, who alternate hitting shots to you at the net. If the shot comes low, get down low by bending your knees, and bump the ball deep and down the middle of the backcourt. If the ball comes at least shoulder high, volley at an angle to open the court (create an open space in your opponent's court). Hit every shot into the opponents' singles court.

Success Goal = 15 out of 20 volleys hit into the target zone ___

Success Check
• Focus on your opponents' shots, not yours ___
• Step forward; don't retreat ___

To Increase Difficulty
• Have your partners hit setup shots with more pace.
• Have your partners hit most setup shots to your weakest side (usually the backhand).
• Keep score; first player or team to win 10 points wins the game.
• Return crosscourt groundstrokes with down-the-line volleys.
• Return down-the-line groundstrokes with crosscourt volleys.
• Move closer to the net after a well-hit volley.

To Decrease Difficulty
• Have your partners hit setup shots with less pace.
• Have your partners hit most setup shots to your strongest side.

8. Target Volleys

Place a large cardboard box on the court as a target. Start with the target in the deep backhand corner, then move it to the forehand corner, then short and wide to the backhand, and finally short and wide to the forehand side. Your partner drops and hits to set you up with shots to volley toward the target area.

Success Goal = hit each target 3 out of 10 times ___

✔ Success Check
• Keep your hand and racket forward together ___
• Open the racket face slightly ___
• Aim for the target area—not the target itself ___

To Increase Difficulty
• Alternately hit forehand and backhand volleys without changing grips
• Move the targets to different areas on the court.

To Decrease Difficulty
• Use bigger targets.
• Use court areas instead of boxes as targets (right forecourt, right backcourt, left forecourt, left backcourt).

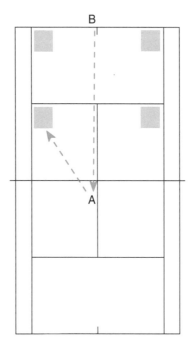

9. Advancing Volleys

You and your partner take positions in the middle of the court behind opposite service lines. Either player puts a ball in play, then both players keep the ball in play by hitting volleys and moving one step closer to the net after each volley. When either player misses, both move back to their respective baselines to restart the drill. The emphasis is on quick reaction and short backswings.

Success Goal = consecutive volleys without a miss until players are within 1 step of the net ___

✔ Success Check
• Put both hands on the racket between shots ___
• Keep your arms extended forward ___
• Block the ball; don't swing at it ___

To Increase Difficulty
• Start from a position halfway between the service line and the baseline.

To Decrease Difficulty
• Have one player feed shots without attempting to return volleys hit by his or her practice partner, then reverse roles.

10. Consecutive Partner Volleys

You and your partner stand about 15 feet from the net, on opposite sides of the net. Count the number of consecutive shots hit to each other using only volleys. Begin the drill hitting soft, controlled volleys. Gradually pick up the pace as long as you can control the ball.

Success Goal = 15 consecutive shots between you and your partner ___

Success Check
• Use a short punch at the ball ___
• Recover quickly ___

To Increase Difficulty
• Stand 2 steps closer to the net.
• Hit only crosscourt (or only down-the-line) volleys.
• Hit only forehand (or only backhand) volleys.
• Move forward 1 step with each successful volley.

To Decrease Difficulty
• Count shots that bounce in front of either you or your partner before you can volley them as good ones.

11. Defend Your Turf

Stand in one service court near the net and defend the area between the singles sideline and the center service line with volleys put into play by your practice partner. Return shots into your opponent's singles court.

Success Goal = return 15 out of 20 shots ___

Success Check
- Keep the racket in front of your body with the racket head up ___
- Bounce on your toes between shots ___

To Increase Difficulty
- Defend the area between the doubles sideline and the center service line.

To Decrease Difficulty
- Have your partner feed balls only to your forehand side.
- Your shots may land within the singles or doubles boundaries.

12. Volley–Volley Up

Stand at the service line opposite your partner, who is at the other service line. Keep the ball in play hitting consecutive volleys. With each volley, bump the ball up into the air to yourself, then hit it across the net to your partner, who does the same thing.

This drill helps you develop touch and take speed off of the ball. Sometimes touch and change of pace are just as effective as power.

Success Goal = 6 consecutive exchanges ___

Success Check
• Catch the ball on your strings as if it were an egg you don't want to break ___
• Hold the racket more loosely than normal ___

To Increase Difficulty
• Conduct the drill using only backhands.

To Decrease Difficulty
• Have only one partner execute the bump volleys.

13. Three's Company

Take a position just inside the service line against two players standing in the opposite service courts, each near their respective singles sidelines. Keep the ball in play using volleys, alternating shots between the players across the net. Change positions every 3 minutes.

Success Goal = 9 consecutive volleys ___

Success Check
• Be aware of racket face position ___
• Make contact in front and to the side of your body ___

To Increase Difficulty
• Have your partners on the opposite side stand in their respective alleys.

To Decrease Difficulty
• Have your partners on the opposite side stand nearer the center of the court.

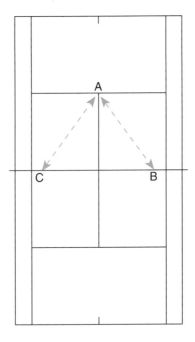

14. Hand-Behind-the-Back Volleys

Take a volleying position at the net, with a partner at the opposite baseline. Hold your racket with a Continental grip; put the other hand behind your back. Keep the ball in play using the Continental grip; keep your other hand out of the way (to avoid the temptation of changing grips, and to build strength in the forearm).

Success Goal = 3 minutes of hitting without changing grips or using the other hand to help ___

Success Check
• Position your wrist on top of the racket handle ___
• Keep the racket in front of your body ___
• Hold the racket tight on impact ___

To Increase Difficulty
• Put a coin between your racket and your little finger; if it falls out, you have changed grips.

To Decrease Difficulty
• Hold your free hand at your side rather than behind your back.

15. Wall Volleys

Stand 15 feet from a rebound net or wall and keep the ball in play against the wall, hitting volleys only. This is a difficult drill. Start out hitting with just enough force to make the ball come back to you. Recover quickly after each hit. You won't have time to change grips.

Success Goal = 12 consecutive volleys ___

Success Check
• Move your hands quickly ___
• Don't let the racket turn in your hand ___
• Use the Continental grip ___

To Increase Difficulty
• Alternately hit forehand and backhand volleys.

To Decrease Difficulty
• Practice groundstrokes against the wall and occasionally move in for a series of volleys.

16. Volleys Win!

Play a set against your practice partner using standard rules, with this exception: Either player who wins a point with a volley wins the game. Regardless of the score, the game is over if you or your opponent win a point with a volley. Caution: Use good judgment when going to the net. Advance to a volleying position because your opponent is in trouble, not to take a wild chance on winning a game.

Success Goal = win at least 2 games by hitting a winning volley ___

Success Check

• Go to the net following a short shot hit by your opponent ___
• Keep the racket head up and in front of you while you move forward ___

To Increase Difficulty

• Play a set in which games can only be won by hitting a volley or by taking a position inside the service line during a point. Replay all other points.
• Play a set in which only one player wins games by hitting winning volleys. Change roles in the next set.

VOLLEY SUCCESS SUMMARY

One of the marks of a complete tennis player is the ability to play the entire court, including the net. The more you practice volleys, the more comfortable you will be in the forecourt area. Work toward developing a variety of volleys, just as you try to develop a variety of groundstrokes.

Before learning how to hit the lob in the next step, have your practice partner or an instructor check the Keys to Success fundamental volley skills illustrated in Figures 4.1 and 4.2. Use a short backswing, step forward, make early contact, and keep a tight grip. Be aggressive. When you are in a position to hit volleys, think about attacking, not defending.

Focus on the ball and try to follow it all the way to your strings. Everything happens in a hurry at the net, so be ready for action. Even if you hit what you think is a winning volley, don't relax. Expect every volley to come back.

STEP 5

LOB: SURVIVING THE POINT

Denver quarterback John Elway can loft a touchdown pass over a defender's head and into the arms of a receiver with remarkable precision. Steffi Graf can lob a tennis ball over an opponent's outstretched racket with equal skill. If you can hit groundstrokes consistently, you are ready to hit lobs.

The lob is one of the game's most valuable shots, but one that players seldom take time to practice or refine. The lob is a high, arching shot with fundamentals not very different from a forehand or backhand groundstroke. It simply goes higher, softer, and deeper into the backcourt than most groundstrokes (see Diagram 5.1).

Why Is the Lob Important?

This shot is effective as an offensive weapon, as a defensive technique, and as a way to keep your opponent off balance. The lob isn't something you use only when you are in trouble; you should use it any time it can help you win a point—this is usually more often than most players realize. Try it occasionally, even if it costs a point. If nothing else, surprise your opponent. If there is never any threat of a lob, the other player anticipates that you are going to drive the ball with normal groundstrokes.

Lob

Hold the racket as you would for any groundstroke; no special grip is required for the lob. If a shot comes to your forehand side, use the forehand grip you have been practicing for groundstrokes. Change to the Eastern or two-handed backhand to hit lobs from the opposite side of your body.

The offensive lob is designed to win the point by using a shot your opponent does not expect. For example, with the other player you would try to hit a passing shot (one that passes the other player), but since this shot might be anticipated, an offensive lob would catch your opponent off-guard, going overhead for a winner.

Make your preparation look like that for any other shot in your groundstroke collection. If you give the preparation a different look, the other player will anticipate what you are up to and get into a position to smash your lob.

Just before you make contact with the ball, rotate your wrist so that the racket face opens slightly to the sky. Although some advanced players occasionally hit a topspin lob, most of the time the shot will be hit flat (without spin) or with backspin. The opened

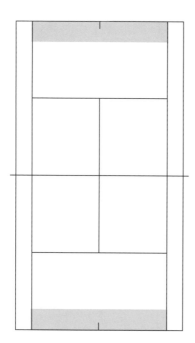

Diagram 5.1 Target area for lobs.

racket face creates backspin. The point of contact may be farther back in relationship to your body than on other shots because you are returning a forcing shot and because if you can wait another fraction of a second, your opponent will be committed even further toward the net.

With the open face and a low-to-high swing, lift the ball upward and aim it high enough to clear your opponent's outstretched racket. The ball should be hit high enough so that it cannot be reached before the bounce and deep enough so it cannot be reached after the bounce. Place the ball to the backhand side whenever possible. If you make a mistake, make it by hitting too high or too deep, not by hitting too low or too short. The penalty for hitting low or short lobs is usually an overhead smash winner by your opponent.

Follow through in the direction you are attempting to hit the ball. The follow-through may not be as complete as on normal groundstrokes, but do not deliberately restrict this part of the stroke. Hold your racket firmly, keep your wrist steady, and try to carry the ball on the strings as long as possible. If you think too much of shortening the follow-through, you may begin to slow down the racket before contact. If that happens, the lob would fall short. Figures 5.1 and 5.2 illustrate the keys to hitting effective lobs.

After a successful offensive lob, move forward to the service line (see Diagram 5.2). If your opponent does get to the ball, he or she will return it with a lob. If you stay on your baseline, you lose your offensive position. From the service line you have time to move closer to the net for a point-ending smash off a short lob. If your lob is returned with a lob deep into your backcourt, you are still in a position to move back and hit a smash after the ball has bounced on your side of the court.

Just as with offensive lobs, hitting defensive lobs does not require a special grip. You may have to hold the racket tighter to withstand the force of an opponent's smash, but hold it with either a backhand or forehand grip as you would for other groundstrokes.

When you hit a defensive lob you are probably either running, out of position, off balance, or generally in trouble. Technique is not quite as important when you are scrambling to stay alive in a rally, but technique should not be overlooked entirely. Anytime you are in trouble on the tennis court, shorten your swing. Sometimes the backswing used in re-

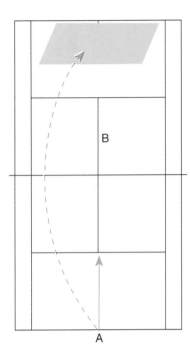

Diagram 5.2 After a successful lob, follow your shot to the service line to get ready for the return.

turning a smash or any other hard-hit shot looks almost like a volley motion. So take a short backswing when you hit a defensive lob. If the other player has hit the ball hard enough, you may be able to just block the ball upward to return it. Again, open the racket face a bit as you make contact. Lift the ball; get it well into the air so you will have enough time to recover and get back into position for the next shot.

If you can, follow through, but don't worry about it unless you are having problems. The follow-through will be upward, and across your body, in that order. A full follow-through will help you get the feel of gently lifting the ball into the air and deep into the backcourt. But if you are really in trouble, get the ball back any way you can to survive the point.

Returning the Lob

If you are at the net and your opponent tries to lob over your head, you can use three possible strategies. If you can let the ball bounce without losing your offensive position in the forecourt, play the shot after it has bounced and return the lob with an overhead smash (a hard, powerful stroke hit from an over-the-head racket position; see Step 6). If you are very

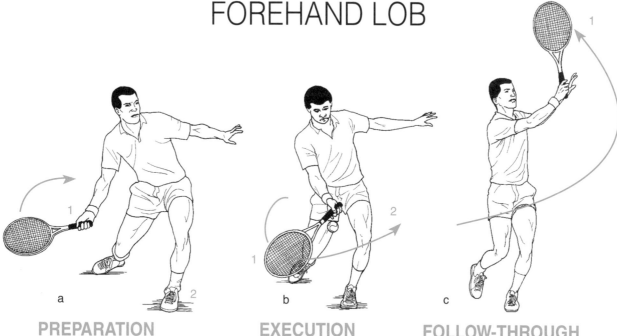

Figure
5.1

KEYS TO SUCCESS

FOREHAND LOB

a   b   c

PREPARATION

1. Forehand grip __
2. Run and plant foot __
3. Short backswing (defensive lob) __
4. Full backswing (offensive lob) __

EXECUTION

1. Open racket face __
2. Low-to-high swing __
3. Lift ball (offensive lob) __

FOLLOW-THROUGH

1. Finish with racket high __
2. Point to target (offensive lob) __

close to the net and the lob is short, move in and put it away with a winning smash.

If, by letting the ball bounce, you would lose your attacking position, play the ball while it is in the air. If you are in a comfortable position, go for a winning volley. If not, return it deeply into your opponent's court with a controlled smash.

If you cannot hit the ball while it is in the air, turn immediately and sprint in the direction of the ball toward the baseline (see Diagram 5.3). If and when you catch up to the lob, return it with your own lob as high and deep as you can. At this point, you are struggling just to stay alive in the point. Worry more about getting to the ball and lobbing it back than how you look doing it.

When you are in the backcourt area and your opponent lobs, you have two ways to play your shot. The first is to set up and hit a controlled overhead smash into the opposite backcourt. The second is to return your opponent's lob with a lob of your own. "Moon ball" rallies (lobs vs. lobs) happen, but not very often.

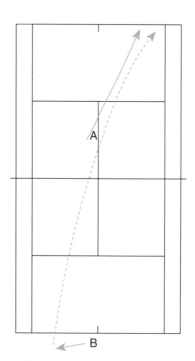

Diagram 5.3 When a lob goes over your head at the net, turn and sprint to return it with a lob from your backcourt.

Figure 5.2

BACKHAND LOB

a

b

c

PREPARATION

1. Backhand grip __
2. Run and plant foot __
3. Short backswing (defensive lob) __
4. Full backswing (offensive lob) __

EXECUTION

1. Open racket face __
2. Low-to-high swing __
3. Lift ball (offensive lob) __

FOLLOW-THROUGH

1. Finish with racket high __
2. Point to target (offensive lob) __

LOB SUCCESS STOPPERS

You will know whether you are hitting poor defensive lobs if your opponent continues winning points with smashes from a position near the net. If you never win points with offensive lobs, you are probably not attempting enough of them.

Error	Correction
1. Your lobs are too short.	1. Aim for the back third of the court. Follow through with the stroke. Make errors deep, not short. Take the wind into consideration. If it is blowing against you, hit your lobs harder.
2. Your lobs fall beyond the baseline.	2. Reduce the length of your backswing; the pace of your opponent's shot can be reflected back without too much effort. Check the angle of the racket face at contact. Remember the wind; if it is at your back, don't swing as hard.

LOB

DRILLS

1. Drop-and-Hit Lobs

Standing behind the baseline, drop the ball and hit forehand lobs into the opposite court. Aim for specific areas in the backcourt, such as the forehand or backhand corners. Use a full backswing and follow-through in this drill.

Success Goal = 10 of 15 lobs into the opposite backcourt ___

Success Check
• Use a low-to-high swing ___
• Open the racket face ___

To Increase Difficulty
• Lob over a partner standing at the service line and holding a racket up as high as possible.
• Try the same drill with backhand lobs.

To Decrease Difficulty
• Begin with drop-and-hit forehand groundstrokes; gradually hit them higher until they become lobs.

2. Lob–Smash Warm-Up

Stand behind the baseline and put the ball into play with a lob to a player at the net. Continue the rally, using only controlled lobs and return smashes. This series is frequently used by intermediate and advanced players as part of a prematch warm-up.

Success Goal = at least 1 exchange of 3 lobs and 3 smashes ___

Success Check
• Use a delicate touch ___
• Deflect the smash ___
• Direct lobs to a point between the net and the service line ___

To Increase Difficulty
• Play the point out after the third smash.
• Follow a successful lob to the service line.

To Decrease Difficulty
• Stand 2 steps behind the baseline to put the ball into play.

3. Run and Lob

Have a partner stand at the net and alternately drive shots to your forehand and backhand court corners. Move to the ball and return shots with lobs.

Take short steps to get started, then put your engine in high gear to run toward the ball. Don't worry as much about technique as just managing to chase the ball down and stay in the point 1 more shot.

Success Goal = 10 of 20 shots with a lob that hits in the opponent's backcourt ___

Success Check
• Start off quickly ___
• Run with the racket back ___
• Aim high and deep ___

To Increase Difficulty
• Play the point out after the lob.
• Lob crosscourt when possible.

To Decrease Difficulty
• Have your partner feed shots only to your forehand side; later, only to your backhand.

4. Lob–Smash Games

Stand at the baseline and put a lob into play against your partner, who begins the game in a forecourt volleying position. Play a 5-point game, attempting nothing but lobs and smashes. Change roles after each game. When you hit a successful lob over your partner's head, follow your lob to the service line. Then be ready to move even closer for a smash or to retreat for a lob deep into your court.

Success Goal = play 3 out of 5 games ___

Success Check
- Bounce on your toes before your partner smashes ___
- Try to anticipate where the smash will go ___
- Lob to the backhand side when possible ___

To Increase Difficulty
- Try to protect the doubles court instead of the singles court.
- Award 2 points to the player hitting smashes; 1 point to the player lobbing.

To Decrease Difficulty
- Protect only half of the tennis court—from center mark to singles sideline.
- Award 2 points to the player hitting lobs; 1 point to the player hitting smashes.

5. Lob–Retreat

Take a position at the net. Your partner stands at the baseline and lobs over you. Play the lob in the air if possible. If not, turn and run to the side of the flight of the ball, and return it with a forehand or backhand lob when you catch up to it. Your opponent moves in to the service line and attempts to finish the point with a volley or a smash.

Success Goal = total of 10 lob–retreat points played out
    5 lob retreats ___
    5 lobs ___

Success Check
- Run to the side of a ball you are retreating with to return with a lob ___
- Lob as high and deep as you can ___

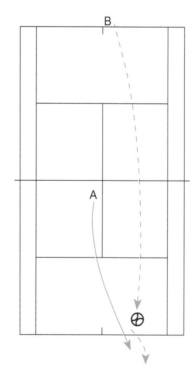

6. Moon Ball Rallies

Hit consecutive lobs with a partner. Use a low-to-high swing, open your racket face, and lift the ball. Each lob must bounce between the service line and the baseline. Keep the ball in play with a moon ball rally until someone makes a mistake by hitting a weak, short shot. Then finish the point with any stroke that will win it for you.

Success Goal = total of 10 points played out ___

Success Check
- Use a low-to-high swing ___
- Think deep ___

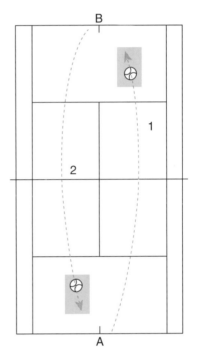

LOB SUCCESS SUMMARY

Test yourself on the lob by asking an instructor or practice partner to evaluate your lobbing technique according to the Keys to Success illustrated in Figures 5.1 and 5.2.

Use the groundstroke grips you have been practicing and shorten your backswing. If you are in trouble, fight to stay in the point even if your technique suffers. This is survival, not a beauty contest.

If your goal is to win a point with an offensive lob, make it look like any other groundstroke until the last second. Then open the racket face slightly and swing low to high. Follow your lob by moving toward the service line for a possible weak return by your opponent.

STEP 6

OVERHEAD SMASH: FINISHING THE POINT

Shaquille O'Neal's slam dunk in basketball makes a powerful statement at the end of a scoring play. An overhead smash in tennis can do the same thing. It's a great feeling to put away the ball and the point with 1 shot. Here's how.

The overhead smash is an aggressive, offensive, hard shot you usually hit from the forecourt area after your opponent has tried to lob the ball over your head. If you are in an offensive position, it can be a powerful, point-ending shot. Some of the fundamentals of the smash are similar to those of the serve, so when you practice one of the shots, you are also working on the other.

Why Is the Overhead Smash Important?

If your opponent knows you have a weak overhead smash, he or she will try to get you to come to the net, and then will exploit your weakness. A good smash makes you a more intimidating opponent and offers another way for you to win points. It is one of the few shots in tennis in which you can let go and try for an all-out winner. A good smash can have a demoralizing effect on the other player, and may help you win subsequent points.

Overhead Smash

Beginners and some intermediates may have to hold the racket with a forehand grip for this shot, but as you get better, start changing to the Continental grip. With a smash or a serve, it allows you to snap your wrist at the top of the swing, and it gives you some alternatives of what to do with the ball.

Because the Continental grip is similar to the one used to hit a backhand, and because you hit the smash on the forehand side of your body, you have to make some adjustments. The main adjustment is rotating your wrist outward just before contact. An outward rotation means (looking at the back of your hand) that your thumb goes away from you, across and down. This pronation allows you to hit the ball flat and with more force than you put on groundstrokes. The inward and downward snap of your thumb and forearm puts added zip on the ball. If you don't rotate your wrist, the shot will have too much spin and probably go off too far to the side. Also, the ball will be hit with less velocity—and smashes need power.

Use a lot of footwork to get ready. Not moving the feet during preparation is one of the most common errors made by players at all levels. Too many players see a lob coming, dig into a fixed position with both feet, then try to hit. The problem is that because lobs are in the air longer than other shots, variables such as velocity, spin, and trajectory may change during the flight of the ball. If you get set too soon, you might misread some of the variables and not make the right adjustments. Take several short, half steps and quarter steps while preparing to hit. Keeping your feet active will help you be in the perfect position to hit when the time comes.

As soon as you see that you can hit a smash, turn your side to the net so that one foot is forward and one is back (as in the serve). Right-handers, put your right foot back and your left foot forward; left-handers, do the opposite. As you hit, push off with the back foot and transfer your weight forward.

Use a partial backswing by bringing the racket directly up in front of your body and to a position behind your head as you prepare to hit. If you were to take a full swing, you would drop the racket down and bring it up behind your back in the pendulum and back-scratch motion. By eliminating the full swing, you can reduce the margin of error. If your position on the court is good, you have enough power to put the ball away or hit a well-placed shot. The full backswing is a more powerful motion, but for this shot it will be less efficient and less accurate than the restricted backswing.

As you draw the racket up behind your head, you might point to the ball with your opposite hand. Pointing can improve concentration and make you aware of your position in relation to the ball, but it is difficult if you are a beginning player. Use the pointing technique only if it helps you hit better smashes; it is not an essential fundamental for this stroke.

The smashing motion is similar to a forceful punch serve. Bring your racket forward as if throwing it across the net, and reach as high as you can to make contact. As you swing, make your weight move into the ball. Hit the ball at a point in front of your body. As you hit, rotate your wrist outward and snap down with the thumb. If you are close to the net, hit the ball with as little spin as you can to get maximum velocity. If you are at midcourt, use some spin to make the ball curve down and into the court. If you are in the backcourt, use some spin on the shot because the distance between you and your opponent is too far for a flat shot to be effective.

Follow through down and across your body. Bring the racket through the stroke naturally, then return it to the ready position for the next shot (see Figure 6.1).

Figure 6.1

KEYS TO SUCCESS

OVERHEAD SMASH

a

b

c

PREPARATION

1. Short steps, quick footwork __
2. Forward with opposite foot __
3. Opposite shoulder to net __
4. Abbreviated backswing __
5. Continental grip __
6. Ball in front of body __
7. Point to ball __

EXECUTION

1. Reach high to hit __
2. Flat hit—no spin __

FOLLOW-THROUGH

1. Continue swing after hit __
2. Racket away, across, down __
3. Return to ready position __

Returning the Overhead Smash

This is one of those times when reaction is more important than technique. Forget Keys to Success, and concentrate on Keys to Survival! Get the ball back any way you can. In most cases, this means returning the smash with a defensive lob.

Try to anticipate where the smash will go so you can get a head start. Most players develop a habit of hitting smashes to the same area of the court. This allows you to make an educated guess on the direction of the shot. Hold your racket even more tightly than you hold it on volleys. You have no time for a backswing; just find a way to get to the ball and block it back with the face of your racket. If you are lucky enough to return a smash, recover immediately. Another one is probably on the way.

If your opponent makes a mistake and hits a smash to you that can be returned with a groundstroke, don't overreact. Players have a tendency to try to blast the ball with a forehand or backhand once they realize the ball is not coming as fast as anticipated. Take that extra time and hit a passing shot.

OVERHEAD SMASH SUCCESS STOPPERS

Learning to recognize and execute a smash is easier if you can compare correct and incorrect techniques. The most common overhead smash errors are listed below, along with suggestions to correct them.

Error	Correction
1. Your smashes land beyond the baseline.	1. Maintain the Continental grip; inexperienced players slip back to a forehand grip without knowing it.
2. You mis-hit smashes.	2. Keep your head up throughout the swing. Try to see yourself make contact with the ball. Restrict the backswing; too much movement causes errors.
3. Your smashes are not powerful.	3. Making contact late (behind your head) and a lack of racket speed at contact cause weak shots. Also, you might point at the ball with the opposite hand, then try to make contact where you are pointing.
4. Your smashes go into the net.	4. Do not let the ball drop too low. Reach up to hit with your arm extended.

OVERHEAD SMASH

DRILLS

1. Shadow Smashes

Take a position at the net and swing through the overhead smash motion without hitting a ball. Turn, draw the racket straight back, and reach high as you swing.

Success Goal = 10 shadow swings ___

Success Check
• Turn your side to the net ___
• Move the racket back quickly ___
• Reach high to hit ___

To Increase Difficulty
• Stand close enough to the net to slap it with your racket as you follow through. Make contact by hitting the entire face of the racket on the top of the net.

To Decrease Difficulty
• Execute the drill in slow motion.

2. Toss and Smash

Stand near the net and toss a ball slightly forward and high into the air. Get your racket back early, reach high, and smash the toss. Keep the ball in front of your body position and do not let it drop too low. Try to make the ball bounce high into the opposite court so that an opponent would not be able to make a return.

Success Goal = 8 of 10 attempts into the opposite singles court ___

Success Check
• Toss higher than you can reach and in front of your body ___
• Start with your racket behind your head ___
• Do not hit bad tosses; start over ___

To Increase Difficulty
• Toss the ball higher.
• Toss the ball slightly behind your starting position.

To Decrease Difficulty
• Strike the ball without trying to hit a smash; add power later.

3. Smash and Touch

Start at the net, move back and swing through the smash motion without hitting the ball, then move forward to touch the net. Remember to move back with your opposite shoulder to the net.

Success Goal = 10 smash and touch combinations ___

Success Check
• Turn your side to the net ___
• Use lots of small steps to get ready ___
• Plant the back foot before moving forward ___
• Retreat with your side to the net ___

To Increase Difficulty
• Start the sequence of swings and net touches farther from the net.

To Decrease Difficulty
• Start the sequence of swings and net touches closer to the net.

4. Lob–Smash Combination

Have a partner hit lobs from the baseline to you at the net. Return lobs with smashes at your partner as many times as possible in a 1-minute period. Reverse roles after each series of lobs and smashes.

Success Goal = 10 smashes placed into the singles court ___

✔ Success Check

• Keep your opposite shoulder to the net until the last second ___
• Keep your head up during the swing ___
• Keep moving your feet until you are ready to swing ___

To Increase Difficulty

• Have your partner feed lobs to various spots on the court.
• Increase the time period to 1-1/2 minutes.
• Play the point out after each smash.
• Hit short lobs with angled smashes.

To Decrease Difficulty

• Have your partner feed all lobs short and to your forehand.
• Decrease the time period to 30 seconds.

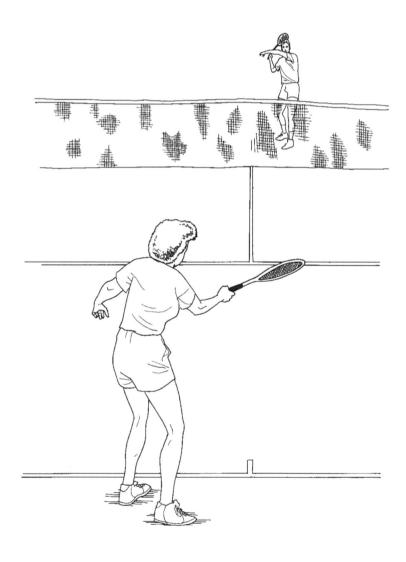

5. Smash to Targets

Your partner hits lobs from the baseline to you at the net. Return lobs with smashes directed at large boxes or similar targets placed in these positions: deep backhand corner, deep forehand corner, just inside the singles sideline on the right side service line, and at a similar location on the left side service line.

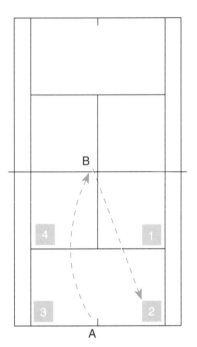

 **Success Goal** = 3 out of 10 smashes to target ___

✔ **Success Check**
• Align your feet in the direction of the target ___
• Attempt more control; less power ___
• Point to the ball with your free hand ___

To Increase Difficulty
• Decrease the size of the targets.

To Decrease Difficulty
• Increase the size of the targets.
• Smash to areas of the court rather than targets.

6. Smash–Lob Games

Take a position at the net and have a partner stand at the baseline, setting you up with a lob. Smash the lob and play the point out. Only the first 2 shots have to be a lob and smash, respectively. The first player to win 10 points wins the game. Change positions and repeat the drill.

Success Goal = win the game when hitting smashes ___

✔ **Success Check**
• Smash wide to open up the court for the next shot ___
• Don't smash to the same spot on consecutive shots ___

To Increase Difficulty
• Count 1 point for winning smashes; 2 points when the opponent wins an exchange with a lob.

To Decrease Difficulty
• The baseline player must return all shots with a lob.

7. Up and Back

Have a partner stand at the baseline with a basket of balls. Start at the net and move back to smash a lob fed to you by your partner. As soon as you hit the smash, move forward to volley a short drive set up by your partner with another ball. Continue for 20 sequences: 10 smashes and 10 volleys.

Success Goal =

10 out of 20 smashes into the singles court ___
10 out of 20 volleys into the singles court ___

Success Check

• Don't hesitate after the smash; go quickly to the net ___
• Retreat for the lob with your side to the net ___

To Increase Difficulty

• Increase the number of shots by increments of 5.

To Decrease Difficulty

• Decrease the total number of shots to 10: 5 smashes, 5 volleys.

OVERHEAD SMASH SUCCESS SUMMARY

For most players, the smash is a fun shot. You can hit the ball hard and finish a point—one way or the other. The key is preparation. Take lots of short, quick steps to get into the right position, get the racket back early, and keep the ball in front of your body. Watch Todd Martin hit a smash and copy his technique. Remember, even though you hit a good smash, it may not be a winner. As soon as you smash to the open court, recover for the possibility of another lob or a passing shot.

Ask your practice partner or instructor to evaluate your overhead smash, using the Keys to Success illustrated in Figure 6.1.

STEP 7

HALF VOLLEY: 9-1-1 TENNIS

There are no celebrity half volleyers. The pros occasionally have to dig out shots that bounce near their feet just like the rest of us. But great players like Argentina's Gabriela Sabatini make a living by being in a position where they don't have to hit many half volleys

The half volley is a shot hit immediately after the ball has bounced on the court. Baseball players catch balls on the "short hop," or right after it bounces in front of them. Tennis players have to play a half volley the same way, but they do it with a racket. The shot is actually a forehand or backhand groundstroke, but the fundamentals are similar to a volley, so it is called a half volley—half volley, half groundstroke.

Why Is the Half Volley Important?

This is a shot you don't want to hit unless you have to. It usually means that you are out of position, have prepared late, or your opponent has hit a forcing shot. In any case, the ball comes hard at your feet and you have to dig it out and get it back. It is emergency tennis (like dialing 9-1-1 on the court) at its best—or worst. Unfortunately, the older you get, the more you find yourself out of position. So keep working on your court position, but also be ready to return forcing shots, when necessary.

Half Volley

Because you have little time to react, this shot requires few fundamentals. Turn your side or at least your shoulders as soon as you know on which side you will have to hit the ball. If you can turn early, your racket will be drawn back and ready early.

You will have no time to take a big backswing, so severely restrict that part of the hitting motion. Also, taking a big backswing leads to a tendency to overhit the ball. All you need to do is block this shot; big swings are not only time-consuming, they are counterproductive.

After you have turned your side to the net, crouch (as though you are sitting on a stool or bench) while you hit. Try to keep the ball at eye level and stay low throughout the shot. As you swing forward, block the ball and try to make contact out in front of your position. Lift the racket head as you make contact, in order to get the ball over the net.

On balls that come at you without a lot of pace, the follow-through is relatively normal. Hit the ball and continue your swing. On fast-paced shots, just block the ball as it leaves the court surface and don't worry about a follow-through. Aim your strings in the target direction, hold tight, and watch what happens (see Figure 7.1).

Returning the Half Volley

Be ready for anything. If your opponent is in real trouble while attempting a half volley, there is a good chance the ball will deflect off his or her racket weakly and set you up for a winner. However, many good players, and a few lucky ones, can turn a difficult situation into an opportunity to win a point. In that case, your opponent's shot will come back faster and with more pace than you expect.

With the half volley, as with any other possible return in tennis, expect the worst. This means hitting your shot and immediately recovering to the ready position for anything that comes your way. If your opponent returns your shot with a weak setup, quickly count your blessings and go for a winner.

Figure
7.1 **KEYS TO SUCCESS**

HALF VOLLEY

Forehand Half Volley

PREPARATION

1. Turn your side early ___
2. Plant feet before hitting ___
3. Short backswing ___

EXECUTION

4. Make contact early ___
5. Hold racket tightly ___
6. Stay low ___

FOLLOW-THROUGH

7. None on hard shots ___ or
8. Finish stroke on slow shots ___

Backhand Half Volley

PREPARATION

1. Turn your side early ___
2. Plant feet before hitting ___
3. Short backswing ___

EXECUTION

4. Make contact early ___
5. Hold racket tightly ___
6. Stay low ___

FOLLOW-THROUGH

7. None on hard shots ___ or
8. Finish stroke on slow shots ___

HALF VOLLEY SUCCESS STOPPERS

A trained eye is needed to spot problems with this stroke because everything happens very fast. Have an experienced partner or instructor watch you for these problems.

Error	Correction
1. The racket turns in your hand on contact.	1. Hold the racket tighter.
2. Your half volleys go beyond the baseline.	2. Just block the ball—do not swing at it or try to fight power with power.
3. You hit too late and the ball goes to the side.	3. Shorten your backswing; you don't have enough time for a full one.
4. You are having to hit too many half volleys.	4. Stay out of no man's land between the baseline and the service line.

HALF VOLLEY

DRILLS

1. Quick Hits

Stand in the middle of the court 1 step behind the service line. Drop and hit 20 shots on your forehand side, trying to make contact as quickly after the ball bounces as possible. Listen for the "bang-bang" sound of the ball hitting the court, then being hit by your racket strings.

Success Goal = 15 of 20 attempts hit into the opposite singles court ___

Success Check
• Use a short backswing ___
• Lift the ball ___
• Listen for the "bang-bang" sound ___

To Increase Difficulty
• Direct your half volleys to specific areas of the court.

To Decrease Difficulty
• Begin by dropping and hitting normal forehand groundstrokes. Gradually decrease the time between dropping and hitting the ball.

2. Play Shortstop

Take a position 1 step behind the baseline without your racket. Have your partner stand at the net and drive balls toward you so they bounce several times before reaching you. Move into a position in line with the ball with knees bent and hands down. Field the tennis ball grounders just as a shortstop would field baseballs. Learning to handle tennis balls after short hops will get you ready for half volleys.

Success Goal = 10 consecutive fielding plays without an error ___

Success Check
• Bend your knees more than your waist ___
• Watch the ball into your hands ___

To Increase Difficulty
• Toss the ball back to your partner on one bounce and let him or her hit groundstrokes that bounce several times before they reach you.

To Decrease Difficulty
• Have your partner toss balls to you rather than hitting them with a racket.

3. No Man's Land Rally

Take a position between the baseline and the service line. Keep the ball in play against a partner in the same position on the opposite side of the net with controlled shots, including those hit with the short-hop half volley. Although this is not a good position for match play, it forces you to practice shots that may help your game later.

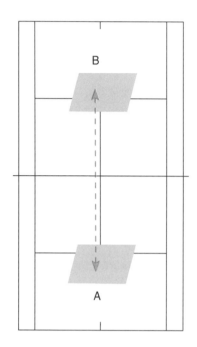

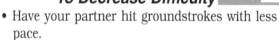 **Success Goal** = return 4 of 5 attempted half volleys ___

Success Check
- Crouch before hitting ___
- Block the ball; don't swing ___
- Try to see the ball hit your racket strings ___

To Increase Difficulty
- Have your partner hit groundstrokes with more pace.
- Vary your position between the service line and baseline.

To Decrease Difficulty
- Have your partner hit groundstrokes with less pace.
- Stand deeper in the court, near the baseline.

4. Quick Time Rally

Take a position between the baseline and the service line. Keep the ball in play against a partner positioned very close to the net. Your partner's shots will be returned to you even faster than during the No Man's Land Rally in Drill 3. Work on anticipating where the next shot will be directed. Technique is not as important as quickness.

 **Success Goal** = return 3 of 5 attempted half volleys ___

Success Check
- Hold your racket tightly just before contact ___
- Scrape the court with your racket when necessary ___

To Increase Difficulty
- Move closer to or inside the service line to return your opponent's shots with half volleys.

To Decrease Difficulty
- Move 2 steps deeper into your own court to give yourself more time to hit and recover.

5. Close Shave Service Returns

Have a partner practice the serve while you practice returns from a position 1 step behind the service line. Change roles after 20 serves. This drill not only helps your half volley, but it also improves your serve return and quickness.

Success Goal = 3 half volleys into singles court out of 10 attempts ___

Success Check
- Turn your shoulders quickly ___
- Use a restricted backswing ___
- Step forward with your opposite foot (if you have time) ___

To Increase Difficulty
- Stand on the service to return serves.
- Have your partner serve with more pace.

To Decrease Difficulty
- Stand 3 steps behind the service line.
- Have your partner serve with less pace or from 2 steps behind the baseline.

6. Hot Seat Half Volleys

Stand on the service line with a player at the baseline behind you with a basket of balls. Two players stand at the net opposite you. The baseline player sets up the volleyers (C, D), who hit shots directly at you. Dig out as many shots as you can with volleys and half volleys.

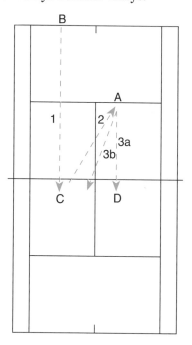

Success Goal = return 2 out of 10 attempts ___

✔ Success Check
- Be aggressive; don't be nice ___
- Watch your opponents' racket faces ___
- Stay low ___
- Survive ___

To Increase Difficulty
- Stand just in front of the service line.

To Decrease Difficulty
- Stand 2 steps behind the service line.

7. Baseline Half Volleys

Your partner stands at the net with a basket of balls and drives balls hard at your feet on the baseline. Hold your racket tightly and shorten your backswing. Other than that, forget technique and fight to keep the ball in play with half volleys.

Success Goal = 4 half volleys out of 10 attempts ___

✔ Success Check
- Turn quickly and block the shot ___
- Scrape the court with your racket, if necessary ___

To Increase Difficulty
- Stand 1 step in front of the baseline.

To Decrease Difficulty
- Have your practice partner stand farther from the net to feed you balls.

HALF VOLLEY SUCCESS SUMMARY

More than any other stroke, the test of your half volley technique is whether the ball goes back over the net. Keep your eyes wide open, turn your side early, block the ball, hold your racket tightly, and swing the racket low enough to dig the ball out of the court. Remember, this shot will test your reflexes and willpower more than your technique. Nevertheless, ask someone to use the Keys to Success checklist illustrated in Figure 7.1 to evaluate your ability to hit half volleys.

STEP 8

DROP SHOT: DECEIVING YOUR OPPONENT

Fans pay money to watch Greg Norman drive a golf ball 350 yards, but Greg makes his money with a delicate putting touch. In tennis, a delicately hit drop shot is just as effective as a spectacular serve, volley, or smash. It's time to add the drop shot to your collection of skills.

A drop shot floats softly into the opponent's forecourt area and bounces twice before he or she can get to it. This kind of shot usually follows a series of strokes and comes when the opponent expects a hard and deep return. Although it can be used by any player, a well-hit drop shot is a relatively sophisticated stroke used by intermediate and advanced players.

Why Is the Drop Shot Important?

This shot is effective against players who are out of position, out of shape, or who do not cover the court well. It also works well against opponents who are tired, lazy, or both. If you use the shot often enough, your opponent's concern that you might use it again can make other shots from a similar position on the court become more effective.

For example, if the other player hits a weak shot that bounces inside your service court, you could move forward to appear to smash it deep into the opposite backcourt. Your opponent will probably start preparing to defend this kind of shot. But instead, execute a delicate drop that barely clears the net. Just like other strokes and their variations, this shot gives you one more option and your opponents one more problem.

Drop Shot

The drop shot preparation should look like that for any other shot you might hit from the forecourt. To disguise the shot, don't exaggerate the backswing, delay the stroke, or change footwork or facial expression. Hold the racket firmly, but not overly tight, open the racket face slightly, and delicately slide it under the ball as you make contact.

Start with the racket head above waist level and swing down in front of the ball. The high-to-low swing and the open racket face should give the shot a bit of backspin. Abbreviate your follow-through on shots played after the bounce. Drop volleys (drop shots hit with volleys) are also more effective if the follow-through is abbreviated. Whatever you do, avoid trying a drop shot from a position behind your baseline. Your opponent has too much time to read the shot and get to the ball.

Hit the drop shot so that the ball falls downward as it clears the net. Barely clearing the net is effective, but not absolutely necessary. Avoid hitting the ball so that it travels too far toward your opponent after the bounce. Putting backspin on the ball by hitting with an open racket face should make it bite into the court and slow down (see Figure 8.1).

Expect the other player to reach the ball and to return it. If it isn't returned, you win the point; if it is, you should be near the net and ready to volley the ball for a winner. Hitting drop shots on consecutive points may be a good idea if the other player has to work hard to get to the ball on the first drop shot.

Figure
8.1

KEYS TO SUCCESS

DROP SHOT

a   b   c

PREPARATION

1. Forehand or backhand grip ___
2. Disguise the shot ___

EXECUTION

1. Open racket face ___
2. High-to-low swing ___

FOLLOW-THROUGH

1. Abbreviated swing after contact ___
2. Recover for next shot ___

Returning the Drop Shot

Many players telegraph drop shots by changing their stroke or their body language. By observing how your opponent prepares and hits this shot compared to the way he or she normally hits groundstrokes, you may be able to outguess your opponent and get to the ball for a winner.

If a player is in the forecourt and in a position to hit a variety of shots, you must at least be aware that the drop shot is a possibility. This is especially true if you are well behind the baseline or wide to either side. Make your opponent prove that he or she can hit this shot before trying to anticipate it. One successful drop is normal. If you keep getting beaten by the shot, then it's your fault.

As soon as you recognize the drop shot is coming (see Diagram 8.1), blast off toward the ball as fast as you can. If you get to the ball quickly, put it down the line for a winner. If you have to stretch at the last second, consider putting the ball over your opponent's head with a lob. This is difficult, but may be your best shot because the racket face is already in the up position and your weight can carry the ball deep. If you attempt the lob and it goes short, duck to avoid the inevitable slam.

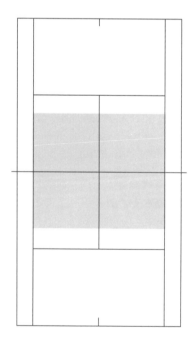

Diagram 8.1 Target areas for drop shots.

DROP SHOT SUCCESS STOPPERS

You will know if your drop shot is effective by the number of times you use it successfully. Many times the success of the shot depends on when it is used, rather than on the technique you use to hit it.

Error	Correction
1. You are hitting the drop shot too hard or too deep.	1. Don't swing hard; this is a touch shot, not a power shot.
2. The drop shot goes too high over the net.	2. Reduce the angle of the racket face. Putting the ball high into the air gives the other player too much time to get to it.
3. Your shot falls into the net.	3. Use the shot from the forecourt; trying it from the baseline is too risky unless you have a big lead in the match. Open the racket face for back spin; do not hit the ball flat (without spin).

DROP SHOT

DRILLS

1. Drop-and-Hit Drop Shots

Stand at the service line, drop the ball, and hit it after the bounce with a drop shot into the opposite service court. Use your forehand to practice this drill; make it look as much like your normal forehand swing as possible.

Success Goal = 8 out of 10 attempts into the service court ___

Success Check
• Use the Eastern forehand grip ___
• Disguise the shot ___
• Use a delicate touch ___
• Swing high to low for backspin ___

To Increase Difficulty
• Make the ball bounce at least twice before it crosses the opposite service line.

To Decrease Difficulty
• Stand halfway between the service line and the net.

2. Drop Shot Setups

Stand in the center of the court and just behind the service line. Have your partner, on the other side, drop and hit shots that bounce between you and the net. Return each setup with a drop shot.

 **Success Goal** = 5 out of 10 drop shot attempts returned to the service court ___

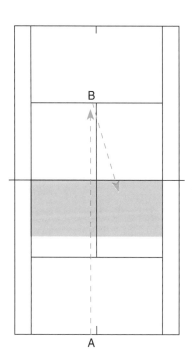

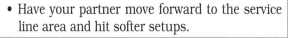 **Success Check**
- Slightly relax your grip ___
- Bump the ball as if it is an egg you don't want to break ___
- Watch your shot for backspin ___

To Increase Difficulty
- Compete by counting 1 point for each successful setup, and 1 point for each successful drop shot.
- Have your partner hit setups randomly to your forehand and backhand sides.

To Decrease Difficulty
- Have your partner move forward to the service line area and hit softer setups.

3. Drop Shot Points

Stand just behind your service line and have a partner stand at the opposite baseline. Your partner drops and hits 10 shots into the forecourt. You return with a drop shot and play the point out.

Success Goal = win at least half the points played ___

Success Check
- Vary the location of your drop shot ___
- Anticipate what your partner will do with the next shot ___

To Increase Difficulty
- Have your partner start the drill 1 step in front of the baseline.

To Decrease Difficulty
- Change the rules to allow the player at the net to hit any shot. The player at the baseline will not know whether to charge forward after the setup.

4. Short Game

Play a game against your partner using only drop shots. Any ball hit hard or that bounces outside of the service court area is out-of-play. Put the ball into play with a soft, drop-and-hit forehand.

Success Goal = win at least half the games played ___

Success Check

• Use the center of the service line as a base from which to operate ___
• Hit and recover to the center of the service line ___

To Increase Difficulty

• One player hits all down-the-line drops; the other hits all crosscourt drop shots.

To Decrease Difficulty

• Instead of competing for points, work with your partner to see how many consecutive drop shots you can hit.

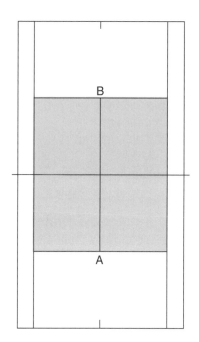

5. Drop Shot Wins!

Play a set against a partner. If either player hits a winning drop shot from the forecourt area, that game is over. Move on to the next game. Don't try the shot just to win a point/game. Try it when you are positioned near the net and your partner is too far away to get to the ball.

Success Goal = win 1 game during the set with a successful drop shot ___

Success Check

• Position yourself near the forecourt ___
• Wait for the right opportunity ___

To Increase Difficulty

• Players must get into position and use at least one drop shot per game.
• When returning drop shots, play the ball after the second bounce.

To Decrease Difficulty

• Call a "let" and replay the point if your partner gets to the ball and returns your drop shot for a winner.

DROP SHOT SUCCESS SUMMARY

The drop shot requires good shot selection, deception, and a delicate touch. Good shot selection means knowing when to use the drop and when to use another shot. Attempting a drop shot from your own baseline is an example of bad shot selection. Hitting a drop shot when you are positioned in the forecourt and when your opponent expects you to drive the ball deeply indicates good shot selection. Use the drop occasionally (even if it results in losing a point) just to remind your opponent that you have a variety of shots in your arsenal.

After you have completed the drills, ask your practice partner or instructor to check your fundamentals, using the Keys to Success illustrated in Figure 8.1.

STEP 9

SINGLES STRATEGY: MAXIMIZING YOUR STROKES

S pain's Arantxa Sanchez is one of the best players in the world because she gets the most out of her ability. She does not have the size and strength of many other pros, but she makes up for it by thinking, hustling, and counter-punching her way into the top ten. Now that you know how to hit, you can decide on the style of play best for you. Some players are more comfortable at the baseline and are very successful developing a strong game based on groundstrokes. They depend on preparation, consistency, patience, and endurance to defeat opponents.

Others would rather advance to the net as much as possible and try to win with strong serves, volleys, and smashes. Power, speed, and aggression are essential for this style of play.

Others can play from any position on the court. These players vary their style depending on the opponent, the kind of court, and the strokes that are working well for them at the time.

Groundstrokes

Good forehand and backhand groundstrokes can keep you in the point, set you up for winners, allow you to apply constant pressure, and make opponents move, make errors, and leave part of the court open. In singles, groundstrokes are the basic tools to help you put together a winning game plan. Use the following suggestions to put your groundstrokes to the best use.

- Move to a position behind the center of the baseline between groundstrokes (see Diagram 9.1).
- Hit most baseline groundstrokes crosscourt.

- Hit most baseline groundstrokes deep into the court.
- From the forecourt, hit shots at an angle to open up the court (see Diagram 9.2).
- Use a shorter backswing against power players.
- Use a shorter backswing on an approach shot.
- Use a shorter backswing against a fast serve.
- Keep the ball low when trying to pass an opponent at the net.
- During a baseline rally, develop a pattern, then break it (see Diagram 9.3).
- If you are weak on one side, tempt the other player to hit to your strong side by leaving part of the court open.

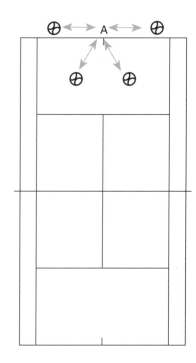

Diagram 9.1 Recover between shots.

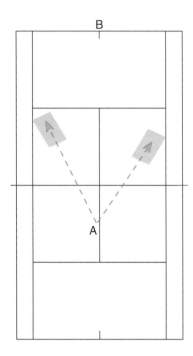

Diagram 9.2 Open the court with angled shots.

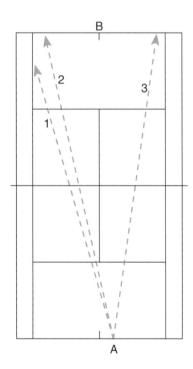

Diagram 9.3 Break a groundstroke pattern.

Serve

The first priority for the serve in singles is to get the ball in play. If you can do this without any problems, then you can begin to move the ball around the ser-

vice court with varieties of pace and spin. If you are not getting at least 70% of your first serves in, reduce the pace.

- Stand near the center of the baseline to serve (see Diagram 9.4).
- Do not waste energy trying to serve aces (service winners).
- Use two medium-paced serves rather than one fast serve and one slow one.
- Serve to an opponent's weakness or to an open area.
- Be careful about serving to the receiver's forehand.
- Serve wide to pull an opponent off the court (see Diagram 9.4).
- Serve deep into the service court to keep your opponent from attacking.
- Use spin on the serve for more control.
- Serve more conservatively when the score is tied or when you are losing late in a game.
- Experiment with a variety of serves during a match.
- When returning a serve, stand near the baseline in the middle of the two extreme angles to which the ball can travel after it is served (see Diagram 9.5).

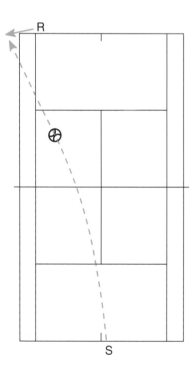

Diagram 9.4 Stand near the center of the baseline to serve. Serve wide to pull your opponent off the court.

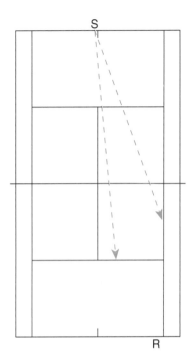

Diagram 9.5 Cover the widest possible angles.

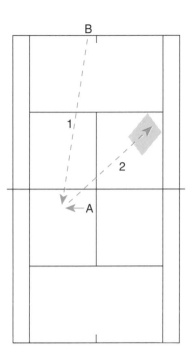

Diagram 9.6 Use a crosscourt volley against down-the-line passing shots.

Volley

Although it is possible to develop a strong baseline singles game, complete players develop their ability to volley from positions all over the court. Look for openings to get into volleying positions. Force your opponent into positions in which part of the court is left open, then move in for the kill with well-placed volleys.

- Stand near the center of the court 10 to 15 feet from the net to hit most volleys.
- Place most volleys deep and into the open part of the court.
- Use a crosscourt volley to return a shot hit down the line (see Diagram 9.6).
- Use a down-the-line volley to return a shot hit crosscourt (see Diagram 9.7).
- When you move to one side to hit a volley, try to move slightly forward as you go to the ball (see Diagram 9.8).
- Move closer to the net after a well-hit volley.
- Use the first volley to set yourself up for a winning second volley.
- When in doubt, volley deep to your opponent's weakest side.
- Expect every shot to come back to you following a volley.

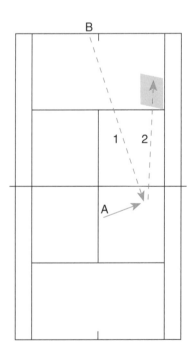

Diagram 9.7 Use a down-the-line volley against crosscourt passing shots.

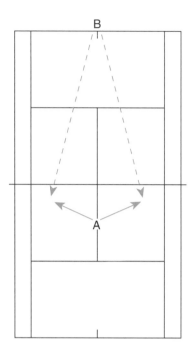

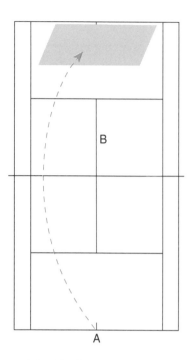

Diagram 9.8 Move forward and sideways to hit volleys.

Diagram 9.9 Aim for the backcourt on lobs.

Lob

The lob is one of the most effective shots in singles, especially against very aggressive players and against those who have weak smashes. Use it at least often enough to keep your opponent off balance. If it works, use it more regularly.

- If you make a mistake with a lob, make it deep rather than short (see Diagram 9.9).
- Use the lob more often when your opponent has to look into the sun.
- Hit most defensive lobs crosscourt (see Diagram 9.10).
- Follow good offensive lobs to the net (stop near the service line).
- Lob at times just to make your opponent aware that your lob is a threat.
- Lob high if you are in a defensive position.
- Lob low when you are trying to win a point with the shot.
- Lob to the backhand if you can do it without risking an error.

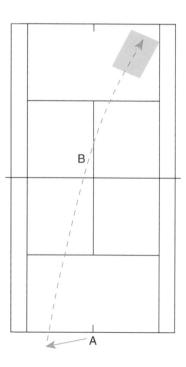

Diagram 9.10 Hit defensive lobs crosscourt.

Smash

As you develop into a full-court player, the smash can become the shot that closes out the point. If you work hard to put yourself in a position to win but cannot put the finishing touch on the point, your work will be wasted.

- Hit a smash after the bounce if you can do it without losing your offensive position.
- Hit a smash before the bounce if you will lose your offensive position after the bounce.
- When close to the net, hit smashes flat (without spin).
- When in the backcourt area, hit smashes with spin.
- Change the direction of a second consecutive smash.
- When you are close to the net, hit smashes at an angle (see Diagram 9.11).
- Hit smashes deep and to a corner if you are deep in your backcourt.
- Do not try to win the point with a smash if you are near your baseline.

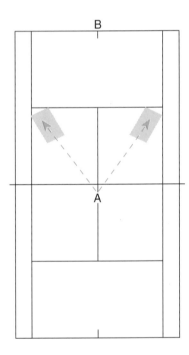

Diagram 9.11 Smash at an angle when close to the net.

Drop Shot

Use the drop shot at least enough to keep your opponent hopping. Let him or her know that you can and will use this shot. Don't overuse it, and follow these suggestions regarding drop shot strategy:

- Hit drop shots from the forecourt area.
- Use drop shots against slow-moving players.
- Use drop shots against players who are in poor physical condition.
- Do not try drop shots when a strong wind is at your back.
- Do not try drop shots against players who can run fast.

General Strategy

Regardless of the stroke being used in singles, keep in mind some general guidelines as you develop a game plan:

- If you win the spin of the racket, choose to serve first if you have a good serve.
- If your opponent chooses to serve first, choose the side against the wind for the first game.
- Hit the simplest shot that will win the point.
- Use your best shot in crucial situations.
- Expect your opponent's best shot in crucial situations.
- In pressure situations, play the ball instead of your opponent.
- If you are having problems adjusting to a surface, go to the net more often.
- Slow down the match if you are losing in a hurry.
- Aim for general target areas rather than lines.
- Do not try risky shots on critical points.
- Take chances on unimportant points (ones you can afford to lose).
- Try something different if you are losing.

SINGLES STRATEGY

Certain situations occur repeatedly in singles play. The more you can practice the situations, the more confident and comfortable you will be when you encounter them under competitive conditions.

In these drills, start each point with the combination of shots described, then play the point out. Repeat the situation at least five times, keep score, change roles with your practice partner, then play the next sequence of strokes.

DRILLS

1. Serve–Return

Have your partner return serves with a forehand or backhand groundstroke. The server should get the ball deep or to an open area of the service court. The receiver should take a short backswing, pivot forward and return the ball deep down the line or deep crosscourt.

Success Goal = total of 10 serve–return points played out

   5 serves ___
   5 returns ___

Success Check

• Serve deep ___
• Use a short backswing on fast-paced service returns ___
• Return shallow serves down the line ___
• Return deep serves crosscourt ___

2. Serve–Short Return

Serve, still attempting to place the ball into the back part of the service court. Your partner returns the ball, using a high-to-low swing to put backspin on the ball and to return the serve short. Direct returns to the open side of the court.

Success Goal = total of 10 serve–short return points played out ___

Success Check

• Observe where the server stands to put the ball into play ___
• Return the ball to the side with the most open space ___

3. Volley Cut-offs

Drop a ball and hit down the line. Have your partner start from a volleying position and cut the shot off at the net with a forehand or backhand volley. The volleyer should move toward the net for the shot. Watch your partner's racket face to anticipate where the ball will be directed.

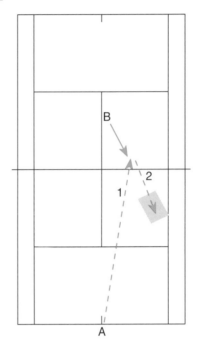

Success Goal = total of 10 passing shot points played out

5 down-the-line hits ___

5 cut-offs from the net ___

Success Check

- Keep the ball low on passing shots ___
- Move diagonally toward the net to cut off passing shots ___

4. Approach Shots

Hit a short shot to one side of the forecourt. Hit it softly and with a little backspin. Your partner moves in and hits an approach shot (a groundstroke hit from the midcourt as the hitter moves toward the net) down the line, trying to put the ball into the corner of the backcourt, then moving closer to the net to cut off the return. It is more likely to be returned back down the line than crosscourt, so protect that side of the court and the middle.

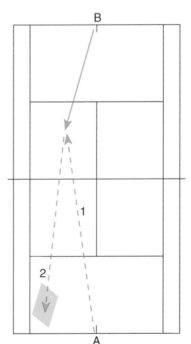

Success Goal = total of 20 shots hit

10 short setups ___
10 approach shots ___

Success Check

- Use a short backswing on approach shots ___
- Follow a good approach shot to the net ___

5. Approach–Lob

Hit a short shot. Drop and hit softly, setting your partner up for an approach. Expect your partner to approach down the line, but be prepared for anything. Expect a passing shot, but move your feet quickly enough to prepare for a lob. Return the subsequent approach shot with a lob, crosscourt if possible. Whatever happens, get the lob deep into the backcourt and move in toward the service line after the ball clears your partner at the net.

Success Goal = total of 10 approach–lob points played out ___

Success Check
• Approach down the line ___
• Lob crosscourt ___

To Increase Difficulty
• Play the points out and keep score until both players win 7 points.
• Allow your partner to start the point at midcourt, dropping a ball and driving it deep to either corner.

To Decrease Difficulty
• Play the first 3 shots with half-speed movement and half-speed shots. After 3 shots, finish the point at full speed.

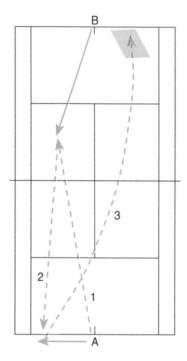

6. Approach–Pass

Set up your partner with a soft, short shot into the forecourt. Your partner moves in and hits an approach shot down the line and deep into the corner. Move quickly to the side and return with a down-the-line groundstroke. Expect your partner to volley your shot crosscourt and move in that direction in anticipation.

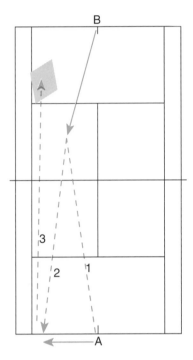

Success Goal = total of 10 approach–pass points played out
   5 short shots, then down-the-line shots ___
   5 approach shots ___

✔ Success Check
• Move forward behind a good approach shot ___
• Return shots down the line unless you get to the ball early ___

7. Attack–Lob

Drop the ball and hit a forcing shot anywhere into the backcourt. Have your partner return with a lob deep and crosscourt, then move in toward the service court area. If the lob is short, move in for the smash to win the point. If the lob is returned deep into your backcourt, move back, let the ball bounce, and hit a forcing overhead smash into the open part of the court.

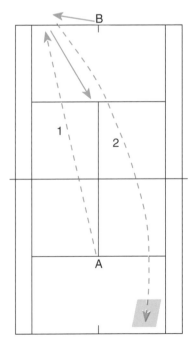

Success Goal = total of 10 attack–lob points played out
   5 forcing shots ___
   5 lobs ___

✔ Success Check
• Lob deep and preferably to the backhand side ___
• Follow a good lob by moving forward to the service line ___

8. Serve-Return-Attack

Serve into the back part of the service court. Have your partner return with a short chip to the forecourt, remembering to use a short backswing and block the serve (don't try to stroke it back). Hit a forcing shot deep into the backcourt and advance to the net, trying to anticipate whether your partner will try a lob or a passing shot. Move in quickly behind your shot and take a split step (squaring your feet) just before your partner makes his or her return. Then move in for the kill, to the side to cut off a passing shot, or retreat backward to return a lob with a smash.

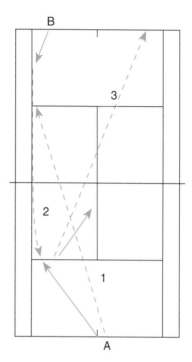

Success Goal = total of 10 serve–return–attack points played out

5 serves and advances ___

5 returns ___

Success Check

• Get the first serve in ___
• Chip with backspin to return short ___
• Watch your partner's racket face to anticipate the next shot ___

To Increase Difficulty

• Continue the drill until both the serving and receiving sides win 7 points.

To Decrease Difficulty

• Play the points with half-speed movement and half-speed shots. Gradually increase the intensity when both players are comfortable with the sequence of shots and court positions.

9. Volley-Pass

Volley from the net while your partner tries to pass you with groundstrokes. Put the ball into play so your partner can hit a groundstroke from the middle of the baseline, moving quickly and taking the racket back before the stroke. Hit your passing shot low. If it goes down the line, look for a crosscourt volley. If your attempt at a passing shot goes crosscourt, anticipate a down-the-line return.

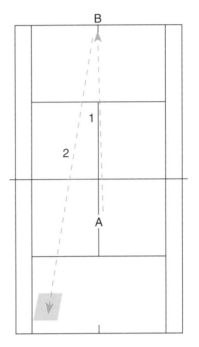

Success Goal = total of 10 volley–pass points played out

5 volleys ___
5 baseline groundstrokes ___

Success Check

• Bounce on your toes before the baseline player hits ___
• Avoid getting into a pattern of hitting passing shots from the baseline ___

10. Suicide Passing Shots

Player A starts in a volleying position near the net, facing players B and C at the opposite baseline. Player A puts the ball into play to player B, who attempts to hit a down-the-line passing shot. A returns the passing shot to C, who attempts another down-the-line passing shot. Player A must volley, then recover quickly to get to the next attempted passing shot.

Success Goal = volley 3 consecutive attempted passing shots ___

Success Check

• Move toward the net with each volley ___
• Plant your foot, volley, and push off in the opposite direction for the next shot ___

To Increase Difficulty

• Increase the Success Goal by multiples of 2.

To Decrease Difficulty

• Allow player A to return the ball to either baseline opponent.

11. Drop Shot–Lob

Start in the forecourt and put the ball into play with a drop shot. Use a delicate touch and try to put backspin on the ball. Have your partner move forward and hit the ball back into your forecourt, concentrating on just getting to the ball, and returning the drop shot with an angled drop shot. Lob back over your partner's head, getting the ball up and over quickly. Keep your racket up and ready in case you make a mistake and have to defend against your partner's smash at close range.

Success Goal = total of 10 drop shot–lob points played out

5 drop shots followed by lobs ___

5 returns ___

Success Check

• Get a quick start off the baseline ___
• Watch your partner's racket face to anticipate the next shot ___

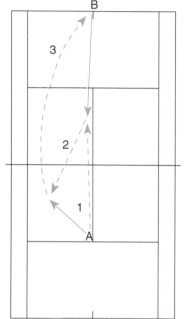

SINGLES STRATEGY SUCCESS SUMMARY

Don't make singles strategy too complicated. Basically, the idea is to get the ball over the net and into the court one more time than your opponent. You have two ways to do that: (a) Keep the ball in play, and (b) hit the ball where your opponent can't get to it. In that sense, singles strategy is more common sense than sophisticated tactics.

Decide who you are on the tennis court. If your strength is at the baseline because you can control forehand and backhand groundstrokes, use that strength. Chris Evert never pretended to be a serve-and-volley player, but she had a Hall of Fame career. Don't pretend you are a power player who can blast opponents off the court. Spend most of your time at the baseline, but work to become a better all-court player.

If you can use your physical strength and speed to hit forcing shots, such as volleys and smashes, do it. That's what Michael Stich and Petr Korda do, and it works for them. Use your spare practice time to develop the consistency and patience to also become an effective baseline player. You may even become talented enough to use a variety of styles.

Points won by patient baseliners count just as much as those won by power players at the net. Playing styles are not good or bad. They either work for you or they don't work. The important thing is to recognize your talents and your limitations. Then get busy becoming a better player, whatever your style.

STEP 10

DOUBLES STRATEGY: SELECTING THE RIGHT SHOT

The selection of shots—when and how to use them—is one of the keys to successful doubles. While speed, strength, and endurance may be more important in singles, factors such as judgment, shot placement, and anticipation can help average singles players become excellent doubles players. Most tennis players become good doubles players long after they have achieved success in singles. You can get a head start in your doubles development by following the suggestions in this chapter.

Groundstrokes

Groundstrokes are necessary, but less important in doubles than in singles. Effective doubles players win with good serves, volleys, and smashes. Forehands and backhands from the baseline should be used as a means of getting into position to win points with more forceful shots.

- Receive serves from a point approximately where the baseline meets the singles sideline (see Diagram 10.1).
- Stand just in front of the baseline against players with weak serves.
- If the server remains on the baseline following the serve, return the ball deep and crosscourt, then go to the net (see Diagram 10.2).
- If the server comes to the net following the serve, return the ball crosscourt and to the server's feet (see Diagram 10.3).
- When you try to pass the server's partner at the net, aim for the singles sideline.
- Attempt to pass the net player occasionally, even if you lose the point.

- When your partner is forced out of position, shift to cover the open court until he or she can recover (see Figure 10.1).
- Let the player on your team with the forehand position take most shots that come down the middle.
- When your opponents are at the net, hit most shots low and down the middle (see Figure 10.2).
- Don't rely on groundstrokes to win in doubles.

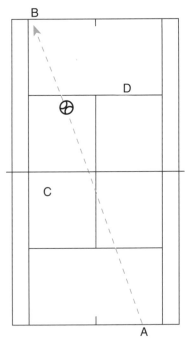

Diagram 10.1 The server (A) stands behind the baseline a few feet from the singles sideline. The receiver (B) stands where the baseline meets the singles sideline. The server's partner (C) stands 8 to 10 feet from the net inside the singles sideline. The receiver's partner (D) stands on the service line between the center service line and the singles sideline.

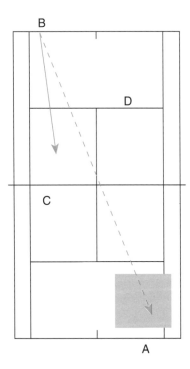

Diagram 10.2 Return crosscourt and deep, then approach the net if the server stays back (intermediates and advanced players).

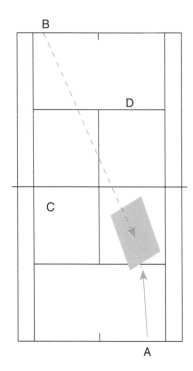

Diagram 10.3 The receiver (B), should return crosscourt and at the server's feet if the server (A) approaches the net (intermediates and advanced players).

Figure 10.1 Shift to cover the open court.

Figure 10.2 Hit low and down the middle when your opponents are at the net.

Serve

Placing the ball in specific locations becomes more important in doubles. Once you figure out where the other players are weak or which spots on the court they leave open, it is important to be able to hit those spots. This is a relatively sophisticated skill and one that requires a lot of practice. The main objective still is to get the ball in play, but putting it into play and in the right places will make things easier for you and your partner.

- Stand approximately halfway between the center mark and the doubles sideline to serve (see Diagram 10.1).

- Serve at 75% speed deep to the backhand or to an open area.
- Serve wide to the right-hander's backhand in the ad (left) court (see Diagram 10.4).
- Serve wide to the left-hander's backhand in the deuce (right) court.
- Let the stronger server begin serving each set.
- Serve down the middle if your partner is good at poaching (moving across to volley the return of serve).
- Use more spin on serves to give yourself time to get to the net.

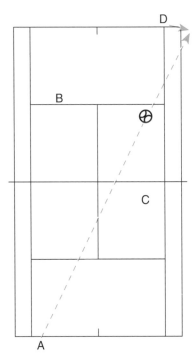

Diagram 10.4 A serves wide to pull a right-hander off the court to make a return.

Volley

Remember that good doubles players can serve to specific spots in the service courts and follow those serves with volleys. The team that gets to the net first in doubles controls the outcome of the point. On the serve return, if you can chip the ball short or drive it crosscourt and deep, then follow your shot to the net, your team can finish the point with strong volleys.

- When your partner is serving, stand about 8 to 10 feet from the net and 2 to 3 steps inside the singles sideline (see Diagram 10.1).
- When your partner serves wide, shift slightly toward the alley.
- When your partner is serving:
  a. Protect your side of the court.
  b. Play weak shots down the middle.
  c. Smash any lobs hit to your side of the court unless your partner calls for the shot.
- In quick exchanges at the net, the last player to hit a shot should take the next shot if it comes down the middle.
- When your partner is serving, stand far enough inside the singles sideline to tempt the receiver to try a shot down your alley.

- When you poach (move across the court and in front of your partner to hit a volley), go for a winner.
- When you poach, move diagonally toward the net instead of parallel to it (see Diagram 10.5).
- Poach occasionally, even if you lose the point.
- Poach more often when your partner is serving well.
- Poach more often when your partner serves down the middle than when the serve goes wide.
- Poach less often if your partner has a good volley.
- Fake the poach at times.
- During rallies, look at the racket faces of your opponents.
- Stand farther from the net against players who lob frequently.
- Play closer to the net against players who seldom lob.
- Retreat quickly, then take a defensive position when your opponents are set up for a smash.
- Stand farther from the net if your partner's serve is weak.
- Shift slightly with every shot to cover the open court. Keep moving.
- Play farther from the net than usual if you are a stronger player than your partner.

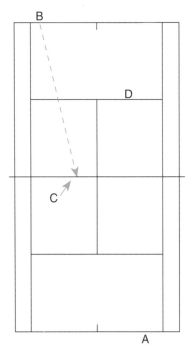

Diagram 10.5 C poaches diagonally toward the net (for more power) to cut off B's service return.

Lob

Although the lob is not a primary weapon in doubles, it should certainly be an integral part of a good doubles team's collection of shots. Having a variety of shots and knowing when to use them can offset the power game of aggressive doubles opponents.

- Lob over the player closer to the net, then follow your lob toward the net.
- Use the offensive lob if the net player poaches often.
- When in doubt, lob deep and down the center of the court.
- Lob low on offense; high on defense.

Smash

An effective smash in doubles is not just important—it is essential. If the other team figures out that either you or your partner cannot hit winning smashes, watch out! Because every serving point begins with one player at the net, that person will be tested early to see what happens on a lob to that side. Also, because the idea in doubles is to take the net away from the other team as early in a point as possible, that strategy will not work if you cannot finish the point with a winning smash.

- Smash the first lob at an angle to the outside of your opponent's court.
- Smash down the middle to create confusion between your opponents.
- Let the partner with the strongest smash take overheads down the middle.
- In advanced levels of tennis, hit smashes at players in weak positions.

Drop Shot

Although there may be exceptions, using drop shots in doubles is not a very good idea. If you do, wait until your opponents are pushed deep and out of position, then hit to the side of the slowest player.

Mixed Doubles

Recreational mixed doubles (a man and a woman on each team) has some unwritten rules. Those rules are mostly don'ts, such as, (a) don't deliberately smash a setup directly at the weaker partner, (b) don't hit too many shots at the weaker partner, and (c) don't try to intimidate the weaker player on a team by hitting hard shots at that player, especially when he or she is at the net. The idea of social mixed doubles is for everyone to have a good time, to get into the action, and to come away from a match in good physical and emotional health.

In tournament competition, however, these rules do not apply. Competitive mixed doubles should be played exactly like men's and women's doubles. Serves should be hit with the velocity and to the place in the service court most likely to produce a winning point, regardless of the receiver's ability. Shots should be directed to the weaker player if the situation calls for that shot. Each player should cover his or her side of the court. One partner should not cut in front of the other unless percentage tennis (hitting the safest, most effective shot in a given situation) would dictate this tactic. If one player poaches too often or hogs groundstrokes, the team's position is weakened by leaving part of the court open for the return. This is also demeaning to the partner.

Given the level of men's and women's tennis today, playing mixed doubles probably means that the team with the stronger woman will win. This is especially true if the woman on the team can play well at the net. In the past, women have been hesitant about developing a net game, but that has changed.

Positioning in mixed doubles should depend on which side of the court each partner can play best. Some people believe that the crucial points are played on the ad court and the stronger partner should line up on that side when the other team serves. Even if that is true, the advantage of having each player play from the side on which he or she is most effective and comfortable outweighs the crucial point theory.

Because mixed doubles usually has the least priority in practice and playing time, use as many shots as you can that create teamwork problems between opposing partners. Moving the ball around the court as much as possible is a good way to manipulate the other team. Lobs are especially effective since one player has to give way to the other, or the partners have to change positions on the court before hitting. Drop shots are usually not a good idea in doubles, but they work in mixed doubles to move opponents out of position and to open an area for a winning shot.

Finally, make the opposing mixed doubles team do what its members do not want to do. If either player is shy about playing the net, make that player come to the net by hitting short shots. If the team is very aggressive and likes coming to the net, use the lob to keep the partners off balance. If one partner wants to dominate, make that player get out of position to do it. If the partners are not used to playing together, hit a lot of shots down the middle to create confusion about who should play the ball.

General Strategy

In addition to selecting shots and practicing situations to improve as a doubles player, consider these ideas:

- Don't assume that a good singles player is a good doubles player.
- Play with someone you like.
- Play with someone who does not criticize you after a bad shot.
- Play with someone whose strengths compensate for your weaknesses.
- Accept your role as part of a team; don't try to dominate the match.

- Left-handers and right-handers usually make good doubles partners.
- Communicate with your partner.
- Stay out of the middle of the backcourt (no man's land) as much as possible.
- Be more aggressive than normal if your partner is much weaker than you.
- Unless you play regularly with the same partner, learn to play the left and right sides when receiving serves.
- Protect the middle more than the alleys in doubles.
- Force the action in doubles.

Just as repetition can help you refine tennis strokes, it can also help you develop your ability to use those strokes in game situations. Following are drills to simulate doubles situations. Players A and C comprise one team; players B and D comprise the other. Practice each situation at least five times, then rotate so that each player begins points at every position on the court.

DOUBLES STRATEGY

DRILLS

1. Serve-Return-Poach

Player A serves, B returns, C poaches and volleys to the open court or to D at the opposite service line. Player A should serve in and deep to give player C the chance to poach and win the point with a volley. Player B, for the sake of this drill, must return crosscourt. However, that doesn't mean player B can't return the serve with a good, low shot that will make the poacher earn anything he or she gets. Player C should poach diagonally toward the net and, as soon as the volley is hit, be alert and keep the racket up for any possible return.

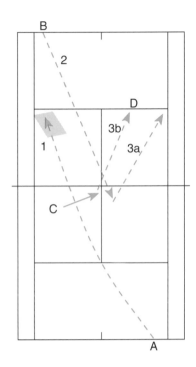

Success Goal = total of 10 points played

5 serves, then poaches ___

5 returns ___

Success Check

• First priority: an "in" serve ___

• Poach diagonally toward the net ___

2. Serve–Lob

Player A serves, B returns with a lob over C at the net, C smashes or moves to cover the other side of the court. Player A has to get the serve deep into the service court. Player B has to disguise the lob until the last second before contact with the ball. Player B should also follow a successful lob by moving in to the service line or closer for the next shot. Player C should get the racket back quickly and move his or her feet faster than Andre Agassi moves his. If player C can't hit the overhead smash, move across the court in the direction of the service line. In that position, the opposite side of the court will be covered while partner player A moves over to retrieve the lob.

Success Goal = total of 10 points played

5 serves, then smashes or lob retrieves ___

5 lobs ___

Success Check

• Use a lower trajectory for an offensive lob ___

• Server's partner [C] crosses and falls back slightly if he or she does not hit a smash ___

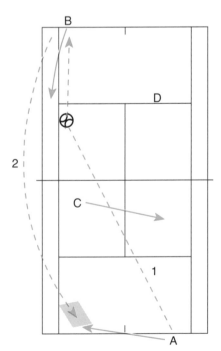

3. Continuous Volleys

Players A, B, C, and D exchange continuous volleys from positions near the service line. The point does not begin until 3 volleys have been exchanged. Players, keep your rackets up in front of your bodies and be ready to move forward for the kill if either opponent makes a mistake. Go for the open shot on the court, or hit directly at an opponent if he or she will not have time to react. Don't hit to hurt; hit to win the point.

Success Goal = total of 10 points played ___

Success Check
• Keep the racket head up and in front of you ___
• Block the ball and recover quickly ___

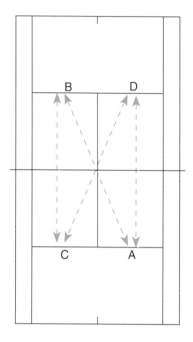

4. Attacking Volleys

Players A and C versus B and D exchange continuous groundstrokes from the baseline. As soon as either team hits a shot that falls into the opponents' service court area, the opponents return the ball deep and move forward to volleying positions near the net. Play the point out. Be aggressive and look for an opportunity to get to a point-winning position.

Success Goal = win 3 consecutive points after moving together to the net ___

Success Check
• Use a short backswing on approach shots ___
• Hit groundstrokes high and deep to keep your opponents on the defensive ___

To Increase Difficulty
• Keep the ball in play 5 consecutive shots before the point begins.

To Decrease Difficulty
• Designate only one team to be allowed to attack after a short shot hit by the opposing team.

5. Serve–Crosscourt Return

Player A serves, B returns crosscourt past C at the net. After player A serves to the backhand or to the open part of the service court, player B takes a short backswing, steps forward with the forehand or backhand, and sends the ball crosscourt and deep. Use this strategy when the server stays at the baseline after the serve. If the server comes to the net following a serve, the return should still be crosscourt, but should fall short so that player A has to reach down and attempt to return a very low shot.

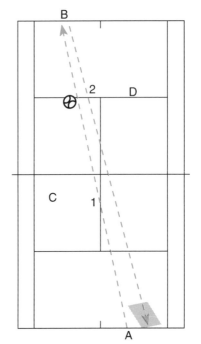

Success Goal = total of 10 points played

5 serves ___
5 crosscourt returns ___

Success Check

• Focus on the ball, not the server's partner ___
• Return deep into the backcourt; use the alley, if necessary ___

To Increase Difficulty

• Hit 5 consecutive exchanges, then play out the point.

To Decrease Difficulty

• Play the shots with half-speed movement and half-speed velocity.

6. Serve–Return–Drive

Player A serves, B returns crosscourt. Player A hits the third shot with a forcing groundstroke. In this drill, player A stays back at the baseline after the serve. If player B returns with a shallow crosscourt shot, player A should be ready to attack with a forehand or backhand drive back to player B. If player B returns with a deep crosscourt shot, player A is still in a position to play the ball with a groundstroke, although it may not be a forcing groundstroke.

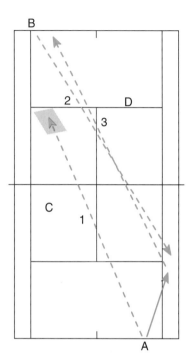

Success Goal = total of 10 points played

5 serves, then forcing groundstrokes __
5 crosscourt returns __

Success Check

- Serve wide to an open space or to a player's backhand __
- Return wide and deep __
- Drive crosscourt and deep __

To Increase Difficulty

- Play each point out and continue the drill until each team wins 7 points.

To Decrease Difficulty

- Play the shots with half-speed movement and half-speed velocity.

7. Serve–Forcing Return

Player A serves to B, player B returns with a forcing shot and advances to the net with player D. Good doubles teams advance to the net early in the point and often during a match. In this drill, the focus is getting player B into the habit of moving toward the net following a crosscourt service return. Once there, player B and partner player D are in an attacking position against one player trapped at the net and one player defending the backcourt.

Success Goal = total of 10 points played

5 serves ___
5 returns ___

Success Check

- Step forward and drive the return wide and deep ___
- Follow a good return to the net for a put-away volley ___

To Increase Difficulty

- Play games in which B and D can only win points when both players are positioned inside the service line following the return of serve.

To Decrease Difficulty

- Establish a rule whereby A (the server) must serve at a slower pace in order to allow B (the service returner) an opportunity to hit a forcing shot and move toward the net.

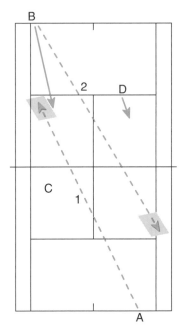

8. Two-on-Two Rallies

Players A and C stand at the baseline and hit groundstrokes to players B and D, who stand at the net and hit volleys. The point does not begin until 3 shots have been exchanged. Once the real point is "on," both teams try to force a mistake by their opponents. If the volleyers return a shot weakly with a ball that lands softly in the forecourt, both players A and C move in for the kill. If players A and C return a volley with a soft floater, players B and D should be ready to move even closer to the net for the put-away volley or smash.

Success Goal = total of 10 points played ___

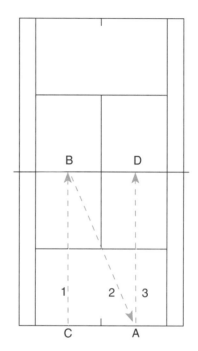

Success Check
- Hit low and down the middle on most ground-strokes ___
- Cut off high groundstrokes with angled volleys ___

DOUBLES STRATEGY SUCCESS SUMMARY

The points in doubles matches begin with very structured shots: First serve into the backhand or open court; return crosscourt; get to the net with your partner as soon as possible, etc. Then things get crazy. With four players, wider boundaries, and inviting angles, that structure dissolves into wild, long, unpredictable points.

While tennis is billed as a lifetime sport, players tend to enjoy doubles more than singles as they get older. Experience, strategy, and shot selection will allow you to compete with players of any age for a long time. Play doubles and have twice as much fun!

STEP 11

MATCH VARIABLES: GETTING THE EDGE

In addition to strokes and strategy, other variables can affect your tennis game. They include different kinds of players, court surfaces, weather conditions, and your own psychological approach to the game. The ability to manage each one can make a difference in whether you win or lose. Here are some suggestions that may help you make those adjustments.

Playing Against Big Hitters

Big hitters (players who rely on power) usually have heavy, flat serves, hard groundstrokes, put-away volleys, and strong overhead smashes. These opponents like to serve, and rush the net. Their asset is power. Their weaknesses, though, may be a lack of patience, mobility, and consistency; it is difficult to hit consistently powerful shots for an entire match. Watch for these weaknesses and be ready to take advantage of them. Most of all, don't be intimidated. These people can be beaten, even if they look better than you do while they are losing.

- Play a step or two deeper on service returns.
- Shorten your backswing on all shots.
- Do not fight power with power.
- Slow the match down.
- Keep the ball deep in your opponent's backcourt.
- Expect to be overpowered occasionally.
- Hit some shots directly at the power player.
- Set a goal of extending each point beyond 4 shots.

Playing Against Retrievers

It can be very frustrating to play retrievers—players who get everything back, but with little pace. They are certainly not intimidating players, and they probably won't impress you with their strokes. If you watch them warm up or play against someone else, it is easy to become overconfident.

The problem is that the ball seems to keep coming back over the net to you no matter how well you are playing. These players know their capabilities and their weaknesses, and they play within their limitations. That attitude is one that all tennis players could use. Here are some ideas on how to play these "human backboards."

- Make the retrievers come to the net.
- Occasionally try to overpower the retriever.
- Attack the second serve.
- Avoid playing the retriever's style of tennis.
- Respect the retriever as much as any other kind of opponent.
- If you have a choice, avoid playing a retriever on a slow court.

Playing Against Left-Handers

Left-handers have a tremendous advantage in tennis. No one is used to playing them and few people enjoy playing against them. Every crucial shot seems to go to the left-hander's forehand. It takes almost a whole set to figure out the left-hander's serve. The only group of players who dislike playing them more than right-handers is other left-handers; it disrupts their games, too.

Left-handers may be discriminated against in society, but on the tennis court they are an elite minority. The number of successful left-handed players seems to be disproportionately high compared to the number of them playing the game. Try these tactics to overcome their natural advantages:

- Regroove your strokes to avoid hitting to the forehand side.

- From the right side, serve wide to the left-hander's backhand.
- Serve down the middle most of the time from the ad court.
- Expect the left-hander's serve to spin to your left.
- Realize that normal put-away shots might go to the left-hander's strength.

Playing on Fast Courts

Good tennis players can adjust to any kind of surface, but going to a fast, slick court is particularly difficult because the ball skids and takes a low bounce. If you have to make such an adjustment, try to schedule some practice time on the court before match day. The entire pace of the game is faster on a fast court. Shots seem to be hit harder, rallies are shorter, and you have less time to get into the rhythm of the match. Try these tactics:

- Get the racket back early and start your swing early.
- Play deeper than usual, especially on the serve return.
- Go to the net on shots that you would not normally follow.
- Expect your opponent to be more aggressive than on slow courts.
- Bend your knees and stay low to hit groundstrokes.
- Don't overhit setups.

Playing on Slow Courts

Adjusting to a slow court is much easier than adjusting to a fast court. On slow, rough courts, the ball slows down and bounces higher than on fast courts. Instead of having less time to prepare for shots, you will have more than enough time on a slow court. You will not be able to put shots away as easily, and you may become impatient because the points last longer. Retrievers love these courts and power players hate them. Everyone can win a few more points by trying these strategies:

- Be more deliberate than on fast courts.
- Be patient.
- Do not waste energy trying to serve aces.
- Be careful about advancing to the net.

- Do not underestimate the retriever on a slow court.
- Get in shape!

Playing in the Wind

Problems created by playing in the wind can be approached two ways. The first is to dread the whole experience, complain about conditions, and blame poor play or losses on windy conditions. The other approach is to try to use the wind to your advantage. It can keep shots in the court that would normally go out at your back, it can add pace to average or weak shots, and it can cause more trouble for your opponent than for you. The trick is to become so involved in the match that you don't even worry about the wind.

- Choose to play against the wind in the first game of a match.
- Toss the ball lower on the serve.
- Keep lobbing to a minimum, especially against the wind.
- Play closer to the net when the wind is against you.
- Play more aggressively when the wind is against you.
- Let the wind provide some of the power on your strokes.

Playing in Hot Weather

Prepare for playing in extreme heat as if preparing to play a tough opponent. Don't ignore the problems hot weather can create. Players who try to prove how tough they are run the risks of cramps, dehydration, fatigue, and not being able to hold onto the racket during long points.

- Don't wear yourself out trying to serve power shots.
- Make your opponent move around the court.
- Keep your racket handle dry with towels, wrist bands, and drying agents.
- Alternate rackets every time you change ends of the court.
- Dress comfortably and coolly.
- Take water to the courts and drink it often.
- Sit in the shade between points and games.
- Wear a hat.
- Use a sunscreen.

Playing Against Superior Opponents

Once a match begins, try not to worry too much about how good your opponent is. You are stuck with each other, so it is best to go ahead and play your style of game. If you walk around in fear that every shot by your opponent will be a winner, you will play below your capability. If you can relax a little and play each point rather than worry about the outcome of the match, you may play even better than you normally do. Superior players frequently bring out the best in inferior opponents.

Playing Against Weak Opponents

On the other hand, do not let your mind wander if you are playing someone whom you should easily beat. Be nice, but try just as hard on every point as you would against someone who is your equal on the court. If you can win 6-0, do it. Never throw points or games in a match because you feel sorry for the person on the other side of the net. If an opponent cannot challenge your tennis skills, make the match a challenge to your concentration. Save your compassion for social tennis.

Playing in Noisy Areas

Noise can be distracting if you are not used to playing where the noise level is high. If people are making enough noise to warrant a legitimate complaint, either tolerate it or ask them to be quiet. If the noise is coming from traffic, from work being done near the courts, or from passersby, learn to live with the noise or choose a quieter place to play. Actually, once you learn to play with a lot of noise, your concentration should improve. If you can concentrate in noisy areas, you can surely concentrate even better in quiet surroundings. Players who learn to play on noisy public courts probably have an advantage over club players used to quieter surroundings.

Playing When People Distract You

People can be a major obstacle to your concentration. Players on adjacent courts talk, hit balls onto your court, and occasionally get in your way or in your field of vision. Ignore them as much as you can without being discourteous. Do not watch their matches if their matches are more interesting than yours. Do not try to keep up with their scores. Play your own match. If your curiosity gets the best of you, get it out of your system by asking what the score is at a time when their match will not be interrupted. People may also be in the stands or near your court watching your match. Keep your eyes out of the stands. Some players find it difficult to keep from glancing around to see who saw that last great shot. If you are counting the house, you are not concentrating on what is happening on your court.

Even the people on your own court can hinder your concentration. Some players may deliberately try to distract you or interrupt your thinking with an assortment of maneuvers. Some of the more popular methods of distraction are stalling instead of playing continuously, talking to you or to spectators, being overly dramatic after a point has been completed, and giving you a bad call just to upset you.

You can handle these situations two ways without totally losing concentration. The first is to decide that nothing an opponent can do will bother you. If you expect trouble from an opponent or even if you get it unexpectedly, make a conscious decision that you will retain your poise and concentration regardless of what happens. That is a difficult task, and it becomes even more difficult if you are losing. Then, even minor irritations become magnified. It is a lot easier to concentrate when you are winning than when you are losing.

If a nonaggression policy does not work, then you might as well confront the person who is bothering you and try to solve the problem before the match continues. Don't put up with distractions if you are going to let worrying about them interfere with your game. If you are thinking about the distractions, you are not thinking about tennis. Stop the match, call your opponent to the net, and explain what is bothering you. If you don't get any cooperation, ask for an umpire or get a ruling from the tournament referee, if there is one. If the match is supposed to be merely a social one, do a better job of selecting opponents next time. It would be better to walk off the court than to become so incensed that an incident or loss of friendship might occur.

Distractions Within

While outside distractions are many, most concentration problems come from within our own heads. We let our thoughts drift; we think about families, jobs, or studies; we worry about people seeing us make a bad shot; and we think about a thousand other things.

Because it is impossible to cut out all nontennis thoughts, at least try to eliminate the most obvious ones. First, play one point at a time. Your opponent is not likely to hit any shot that you have not at least seen before this match. In fact, you have probably returned every type of shot he or she has to offer. All the other player can do is hit groundstrokes, serves, volleys, lobs, and smashes. You might see some shots more often or in different situations, but there aren't that many surprises out there. If you are over-matched, try to win points. If you can win a few points, you can win a game; and if you can win a game, you can probably win some more.

Playing and Concentrating

Concentrating means directing your full attention to a single task or object. Before trying to reach a higher level of concentration, be sure you want to. Millions of players just want to go out, hit the ball, have a good time, and not worry about directing their total attention to the game being played. After all, it's fun to talk with friends, be out-of-doors, watch others play, and relax. But if you want to play really good tennis, you can't think about all these other things.

With so many things not to think about, what should you think about during a match? People can only direct their attention to one thing at a time, so you must establish a priority of thoughts. At the top of the list is the tennis ball. "Keep your eye on the ball" should be more than a platitude. If you are serving, try to watch the ball until it leaves your racket strings. If you are receiving the serve, focus on the ball while it is still in the tossing hand of the server. Follow it with your eyes from the toss to the point of contact, across the net, and into your racket.

Don't worry about whether the serve is in or out until after you have swung at the ball. No penalty results from calling a shot out after you hit it. Continue concentrating on the ball throughout the point; watch it when you and your opponent are preparing to hit, and when hitting.

The second concentration priority is your opponent. As the ball leaves your racket, you will have a second or two to watch where your opponent is on the court and how he or she is going to hit the next shot. Pay special attention to the other player's racket face. If you watch anything else except the racket and the ball, you can be faked out of position. Immediately after the ball is hit to you, be aware of where your opponent is moving on the court.

In this situation, your mind will have to move rapidly back and forth between priority items. You have to be observant enough to know whether the other player is coming to the net, returning to the center of the baseline, or moving to one side of the court. Within a split second your attention must again return to the ball.

The third priority on your think list is the method of hitting the ball. You are much better off if you automatically move into the proper position rather than having to think about it. Because you are preparing for a stroke at the same time you are trying to concentrate on the ball, you cannot think about both things simultaneously. If your strokes are grooved to the point of thoughtless but effective preparation, you can devote full attention to the ball.

As if trying to direct your attention to the ball, your opponent, and your own form is not enough, other factors are worthy of your attention. The score in the game, the set score, the weather, your physical condition, your opponent's condition, and your game plan are all worth thinking about during a match. The time to do that thinking is between points and games, not while the ball is in play.

Become as totally absorbed as possible in the match you are playing. Try to isolate your playing from the rest of your life for the short period of time you are on the court. Forget for awhile that many other things in your life are more important than playing a game. If you can (and want to), create a temporary attitude in which the next point, game, or set is more important than family, friends, or society. You probably can't accomplish this, but if you set that attitude as a goal, any progress toward it should improve your game by improving your concentration.

DRILLS

1. Silent Practice

Practice tennis strokes with a partner for 15 minutes without saying a word. Allow nothing to distract you from hitting the ball. Agree ahead of time on the practice routine to be followed. Any combination of strokes can be used. For example, try 5 minutes of groundstrokes, 5 minutes of volleys, and 5 minutes of serves and returns.

Success Goal = 15 minutes of hitting without talking ___

Success Check
• Don't talk ___
• See the ball; hit the ball ___

To Increase Difficulty
• Increase the length of the silent practice by increments of 5 minutes.

To Decrease Difficulty
• Take a break every 5 minutes, say what you have to say, then resume the silent practice.

2. Silent Sets

Play an entire set without talking, except to call out the score when you are serving.

Success Goal = 1 set completed without talking ___

Success Check
• "See no evil" ___
• "Hear no evil" ___
• "Speak no evil" ___

To Increase Difficulty
• Play an entire match without talking.

To Decrease Difficulty
• Talk during changeovers.

3. "Jam Box" Tennis

Take a radio or "jam box" to the courts and play a match against an understanding friend (only when no other players are present to distract). Turn the radio or tape deck up louder than normal while the match is being played. Try to maintain a high concentration level with the added noise.

Success Goal = 1 match completed with the added noise ___

Success Check
• Block out the noise ___
• Show no reaction to the sound ___

To Increase Difficulty
• Turn up the volume.

To Decrease Difficulty
• Turn down the volume.

4. Take Your Best Shot

Play 10 points in which you set up your practice partner with his or her favorite, can't miss, finish-the-point shot. Keep score, then reverse roles to check your concentration and effectiveness when you are expected to finish points with your favorite shot.

Success Goal = total of 20 points played

2 points won out of 10 attempts when you set up your partner ___

8 points won out of 10 attempts when your partner sets up the shot ___

Success Check
- Anticipate where the would-be winning shot will go ___
- Hit to the open court on setups ___

To Increase Difficulty
- Do not change roles until you win a point after you hit a setup for your partner.

To Decrease Difficulty
- Have the player hitting the put-away shot announce where the shot will be hit.

5. 0-40 Games

Play a set in which every game is started with the score 40-0 or 0-40 against you. Test your ability to maintain concentration and poise by coming from behind.

Success Goal = 1 game won in the set ___

Success Check
- Concentrate on playing points, not games ___

To Increase Difficulty
- Allow the player who is leading 40-0 to serve every game.

To Decrease Difficulty
- Allow the player starting the game down 0-40 to serve every game.

6. Handicap Scoring

Play a set in which a player behind by 1 game begins the next game ahead 15-0. If losing the set by 2 games, the loser begins the next game ahead 30-0; if losing the set by 3 or more games, the next game begins at 40-0.

Success Goal = at least 2 games won per set when starting behind in the score ___

Success Check
- Be aggressive when down in the score ___

To Increase Difficulty
- Have the person ahead in the match serve every game.

To Decrease Difficulty
- Have the person behind in the match serve every game.

7. Obstacle Course Tennis

Play a set with four harmless obstacles (small boxes, rolled up towels, racket covers) placed on your side of the court. Put one obstacle in each service court and two in the backcourt area. Hit your strokes without being distracted by the obstacles on the court.

Success Goal = 1 set completed with the obstacles on your court ___

Success Check
• Focus on the ball, not the obstacles ___

To Increase Difficulty
• Use more or larger targets.
• Your opponent wins the point if his or her shot hits a target.

To Decrease Difficulty
• Use fewer or smaller targets.

8. Plan-a-Point

Plan a point in your mind, then try to play it out against an opponent in a practice set. For example, "I will serve wide to the backhand, pull him off the court; he will return short to my backhand; and I will finish the point with a crosscourt backhand to the open part of the court." Or, "She will serve to my backhand; I will return short to force her to come to the net and hit an approach shot; and I will lob to her backhand corner and follow the shot to the net."

Success Goal = at least 1 point executed in each game played ___

Success Check
• Focus on the first shot of the series ___

To Increase Difficulty
• Announce your plan to your opponent.

To Decrease Difficulty
• Plan only the first shot (serve or return of serve) of the point.

9. Goal Setting

During a practice set, establish goals to improve your concentration. Give yourself 1 point every time a goal is reached during a set. Write down or mentally record the number of points earned when changing sides of the court. Select from the following examples and/or create your own goals.

Success Goal =
a. Hold serve 3 times in one set ___
b. Have no double faults in a set ___
c. Win a game on the 1st game point ___
d. Win the 1st point of at least 4 games in a set ___
e. Return 1 shot no one would expect you to return in a set ___
f. Break your opponent's serve once in a set ___
g. Lose no points failing to return serves ___
h. _____ ___
i. _____ ___

Success Check
• Set realistic goals ___

10. One Free Cheat

Play a set and allow your opponent to make one deliberately bad call during the set. The "free cheat" may be used at any time, regardless of the score. Your job is to retain your poise in spite of being cheated and to continue playing the set as if nothing happened.

Success Goal = win the game in which a bad call is made or win the next game ___

Success Check

• Show no reaction to the bad call ___

To Increase Difficulty

• Give your opponent one "free cheat" per game.

To Decrease Difficulty

• Allow both players to make one bad call per set.

11. Deuce Games

Play a set in which every game starts with the score at deuce. Make yourself play under pressure. Play the ball, not the point or the other player. If weather conditions are not a factor, change sides of the court only once—after you have completed 5 games. Spin a racket to determine serve and side.

Success Goal = play a set ___

Success Check

• Concentrate on getting the ball into play ___
• Be patient; don't try to put balls away too soon ___
• Announce the score before every point ___

To Increase Difficulty

• Add a 1-point penalty if you don't call out the score before starting the next point.

12. Tiebreaker Matches

Play three tiebreakers (review Diagram 2 and the tiebreaker section on pages 5-6). Learning to keep score and to serve and receive in tiebreakers is difficult, but becomes easier with repetition. The first objective is to go through the process several times to learn how it works. The second is to play in a situation where every point is critical.

Success Goal = win 2 out of 3 tiebreakers ___

Success Check

• Start every tiebreaker with 1 serve from the right side ___
• Change ends of the court after each tiebreaker has been completed ___
• Concentrate on the ball, not on your opponent ___

MATCH VARIABLE SUCCESS SUMMARY

Very few matches are played under perfect conditions against ideal opponents. Instead of looking at all of the variables as obstacles, why not see those same variables as opportunities?

Before a match, try to assess the conditions under which you will play. Then decide how you can use those conditions to your advantage. You won't be able to turn every variable into something positive, but at least consider the possibilities. The 1 point you win because you gained a competitive edge might be the point that wins the match.

STEP
12
TENNIS INTELLIGENCE: OBSERVE, RECORD, IMPROVE

People watch tennis matches for entertainment or because they have a special interest in one of the players. But you, as a tennis player, can also watch to improve your game and to scout future opponents. Here are some ways to get more out of your spectating.

Where to Watch

With all of the tennis being played today, you can watch good players in many places. Professional tournaments, television, college and high school matches, and local or regional tournaments all provide settings to improve your game by watching someone else play.

Professional tournaments are probably the most entertaining but least beneficial for the spectator who wants to learn. Professional players are so skilled and gifted athletically, they cannot be compared to the beginning or intermediate player. Many of the professionals have peculiarities in their styles of play that would not be appropriate as examples for lesser players.

Also, there are too many distractions at pro tournaments. A person who goes to one of these events pays a lot of money to be entertained. Celebrities to see, friends to talk with, scores to keep, things to buy, and many other side shows make it difficult to carefully watch the mechanics of stroke production or court strategy. It is not impossible to learn by watching the pros—it is just very difficult. They provide more inspiration than instruction.

Televised matches offer a slightly better chance to learn how to play tennis, but drawbacks still exist. The viewer has fewer distractions, but the nature of television makes observation of many aspects of the game almost impossible. Watching a small screen, it is difficult to get an accurate perspective on things like the ball's velocity, trajectory, or spin, and speed of the players. Everything seems to be miniaturized so much that the subtle aspects of the game are lost to many fans and players.

The best two places to learn by watching are probably at matches between good college teams and at tournaments in your area that attract outstanding amateur players. The quality of play is good enough for you to learn something, the physical capabilities of the players are closer to that of the spectators, fewer distractions are present, and the action is right in front of you. If you are interested in observing matches, watch the papers for announcements of tournaments and matches.

Watching for Preparation

Once you decide to try to learn by watching, what should you watch for? First, look at the way players produce strokes. Start with watching their preparation for shots. Then watch what good players do after they hit shots.

- How do they get ready for the next shot?
- Where and when do they move on the court?
- What parts of the court do they protect or leave unprotected?
- How do they move their feet when preparing for shots?
- How many steps do they take to get from the baseline to a volleying position?
- How long does it take them to get to that position?
- When and where do they plant their feet prior to a shot?

- In which direction do they turn the upper part of their body?
- Do they move toward the ball in a direct line?
- Where is the racket head while they are moving to hit a shot?

Watching to See How Strokes Are Produced

After spending some time concentrating on the players' preparation, try to answer these questions about the strokes they are hitting:

- Where is the racket head in relation to the hitter's waist when contact is made? Is it below, above, or even with it?
- Where do the players make contact with the ball? Is it in front of, even with, or behind the body?
- Are shots hit with backspin, topspin, sidespin, or no spin?
- Do the players swing from the shoulder or the elbow?
- Do they use the wrist (does it flex or extend) on some shots? Which ones?
- When do they transfer their weight during a stroke?
- How high over the net do their groundstrokes travel?
- On the serve, how high do they toss the ball?
- At what point in the serve is contact made?
- What kind of spin is put on the serve?
- Is there a difference between the first and second serves?
- What is the difference?
- How close to the net do the players stand for volleys?
- How much of a backswing do they take?
- Do they crouch to hit some shots? Which ones?
- Where is contact made on volleys?
- Do they use a full swing or restricted swing on smashes?

Watching for Strategy

After you have looked for little things in the strokes, think about the bigger picture of match strategy for a while. Try to figure out what the players are thinking about when they use their strokes.

- Are shots being placed to particular spots on the court? When?

- Does the player who is winning use a different strategy than the one losing?
- Does each player have a game plan? What is it?
- Does one player get to the net more often than the other?
- Does one shot produce repeated winners for either player? What is it?
- If you were the player losing the match, what would you do differently?
- Are the players using percentage shots or do they gamble with high-risk shots? Identify one high-risk shot.
- Which, if any, shots are used more in doubles than in singles?
- Where do doubles partners stand to begin points?

Putting Information to Use

The ultimate test of how well you have observed a match is whether you can answer many of the questions just stated about a specific player after the match has been played. Do you just know who won and remember a few good shots, or can you explain exactly how a player executed the shots and used a plan of attack?

Even if you can remember the details of some players' styles and approaches to the game, it will not do you any good unless you can incorporate some of their strengths into your own game. Don't try to take in so much of someone else's game that you become confused or simply imitate a style for no reason. Find something a player does well that you cannot do effectively or consistently, and copy the way that player does it.

You must be able to imitate the movement of others to play tennis well. People are not born with an innate knowledge of how to correctly hit a tennis ball. Good athletes can watch someone execute a series of physical movements and then imitate them closely. Student athletes must work hard to do what professionals seem to do almost naturally. When you recognize a stroke that looks right to you, capture the total picture in your mind, then transfer the picture from your mind to your body.

Scouting an Opponent

When you watch a tennis match to scout a future opponent, look for things that will show you how to beat this player. When you play together, you will have a better chance of winning if you can answer some of the following questions about the player's game and then take advantage of the information by incorporating it into the match.

- Who is the player?
- Whom did he or she play?
- Who won?
- What was the score?
- On what kind of surface was the match played?
- Is the player right-handed or left-handed?
- In one or two words, how would you describe each stroke?
- Where does the player usually place the first serve? Second serve?
- Where should you stand to receive serves?
- What is the player's best shot?
- What can you do to prevent the player from hitting that shot?
- What is the player's weakest shot?
- What can you do to make the player hit this weakest shot?
- Does the player have any unusual shots?
- Does the player prefer to play in the backcourt or at the net?
- On which shots does the player go to the net?
- What percentage of smashes are hit into the court?
- Can these smashes be retrieved?
- Does the player have a good lob?
- How many first serves go in during a game?
- Is the player in good physical condition?
- Is the player fast or slow?
- Is the ball kept in play for long rallies?
- Is the player honest on calls?
- Does the player appear to concentrate fully?
- Is the player as composed when behind as when ahead in the match?
- What are two things you will have to do to win a match against this player?

If you have all of this information about an opponent, you will be better prepared to plan the match than 99% of the tennis players in the world. Most people don't have the time to get this kind of report on a player before a match. If you do not have the time, consider writing down what you learn about an opponent after you have played a match together. You may play each other again. Use the Postmatch Scouting Form to make notes on a completed match.

Remember that no matter how much you know about another player and no matter how well you plan your strategy, you have to be able to consistently keep the ball in play. Until you can do that, you are not ready to scout other players.

Charting Your Matches

In order to learn exactly what your strengths and weaknesses are, have a friend or classmate chart one of your matches. Charting means recording how points are won or lost. In some cases, what you perceive to be happening during a match and what is actually happening are not the same. During a match, a few good or bad shots may stand out in your mind even though more subtle facets of your game may determine whether you win or lose. Although some coaches and tournament players use elaborate, computerized charting systems, you can keep track of match data with something simple like the following Error Chart and Winning Shot Chart.

Use the information on the Error Chart to improve weaknesses during practice time. For example, if the chart shows that you are double faulting at least once a game, work on a more conservative second serve. If you have too many backhand errors, change your grip. If the lob column shows zero errors, you may either have a good lob or you may never have attempted one during competition.

Any column on the chart with an unusual number of errors indicates that you should practice the stroke more or figure out ways to avoid using the strokes that give you problems. For example, "run around" a backhand because it is weak and turn it into a forehand shot. Or if you continue to lose points hitting volleys, stay away from the net.

The Winning Shot Chart should provide two pieces of information. First, it should reinforce what you consider to be your best shots. If that is true, continue to position yourself to hit those shots during a match. Good players have at least one killer shot to finish points. Second, the chart should indicate the balance, or lack of balance, in your game. Using a forehand for 90% of the points you win may not be bad, but it tells you how much you rely on that shot. Winning points with a well-balanced combination of groundstrokes, volleys, and smashes indicates that you have developed an all-court game. Or you could learn that you are winning points with a stroke you don't particularly like or one that you do not consider strong. If that happens, you may have even more confidence in using those shots in the future.

Postmatch Scouting Form

Directions: Play a set or a match, then complete this form.

Name of opponent _____ Date of match _____

Results of match: _____ Won, _____ Lost, _____ Score _____

Type of court _____ Weather _____

Write one observation about your opponent in each category.

Forehand _____

Backhand _____

First serve _____

Second serve _____

Forehand volley _____

Backhand volley _____

Smash _____

Best shot _____

Weakest shot _____

Speed _____

Strength _____

Quickness _____

Endurance _____

Style of play _____

Right-handed/left-handed _____

Honesty on calls _____

Comments _____

Error Chart

Directions: Tally errors made on the strokes listed in the left column for each game. For example, make a mark each time the first serve fails to go into the proper court. If it has failed three times in the first game, the box should contain three marks (///).

Game

Stroke	1	2	3	4	5	6	7	8	9
1st serve									
2nd serve									
Forehand serve return									
Backhand serve return									
Forehand groundstroke									
Backhand groundstroke									
Forehand volley									
Backhand volley									
Lob									
Smash									
Drop shot									

Winning Shot Chart

Directions: Tally winning shots made with the strokes listed in the left column during each game.

Game

Stroke	1	2	3	4	5	6	7	8	9
1st serve									
2nd serve									
Forehand serve return									
Backhand serve return									
Forehand groundstroke									
Backhand groundstroke									
Forehand volley									
Backhand volley									
Lob									
Smash									
Drop shot									

RATING YOUR PROGRESS

Rate your success by writing the appropriate number in the space to the right of each skill listed. Add the numbers when you finish and check the key that follows to get an indication of your progress.

5=Excellent 4=Above average 3=Average 2=Below average 1=Unsuccessful

1. Keeping score   ___
2. Handling the racket   ___
3. Preparing to hit   ___
4. Forehand   ___
5. Backhand   ___
6. Punch serve   ___
7. Full-swing serve   ___
8. Beginner's volley   ___
9. Advanced volley   ___
10. Lob   ___
11. Overhead smash   ___
12. Half volley   ___
13. Drop shot   ___
14. Using singles strategy   ___
15. Using doubles strategy   ___
16. Adjusting to conditions   ___
17. Adjusting to different styles   ___
18. Limiting self-talk   ___
19. Concentration   ___
20. Persistence   ___

Total   ___

Score	Progress
90-100	Excellent
80-90	Above average
70-80	Average
Less than 70	Below average

GLOSSARY

ace—A winning serve that the receiver cannot touch with the racket.

ad—Advantage; refers to the point after the score was deuce.

ad court—The left half of a player's court as that player faces the net from the baseline.

ad in—A reference to the score when the player serving has won the point after the score was deuce.

ad out—A reference to the score when the player receiving the serve has won the point after the score was deuce.

all—A tie score; 30 all, for example, means that the score is 30-30.

alley—A lane, 4-1/2 feet wide, running the length of, and on both sides of, the singles court. The alleys are in play for all shots after the serve in doubles.

amateur—A person who does not accept money for playing or teaching tennis.

American twist—A type of serve in which the ball's spin imparted by the racket is the opposite of what it would normally be. A right-hander's American twist serve produces left-to-right spin on the ball.

angle shot—A shot that crosses the net at a severe angle.

approach shot—A shot that the hitter follows to the net.

Association of Tennis Professionals (ATP)—An organization composed of most of the leading male players in the world.

Australian doubles—A doubles formation in which the player at the net (the server's partner) lines up on the same half of the doubles court as the server.

backcourt—The part of the court between the service line and the baseline.

backhand—A stroke that a right-handed player hits by reaching across the body to the left side; a left-handed player reaches across to the right side to hit a backhand.

backspin—Reverse spin on the ball, like a car wheel in reverse.

backswing—The preparation for a stroke in which the racket is drawn back before being swung forward.

balance point—The point in the shaft of a racket where the head and the handle are balanced.

baseline—The boundary line that runs parallel to, and 39 feet from, the net.

block—The return of a ball with a very short swinging motion.

carry—A shot that is carried on the racket strings, slung, or hit twice as the ball is returned. Carries are legal unless the player makes two or more deliberate attempts to hit the ball over the net; carries may be called by the umpire or by the player who hits the ball.

center mark—A line dividing the baseline at the center. The server may not legally step on the center mark before striking the ball.

center service line—The line in the middle of the court, perpendicular to the net, that divides the two service courts.

chip—A groundstroke hit with a short backswing and with backspin on the ball. The chip is usually meant to be a shallow shot (not very deep into the opponent's court).

choke—To play poorly because of the pressure of competition.

choke up—To hold the racket at a point higher on the handle, away from the base of the grip.

chop—A shot hit with backspin to any part of the court.

circuit—A series of tournaments at the state, sectional, national, or international level.

closed stance—A position in which the toes of both feet form a line parallel to either sideline.

closed tournament—An event open only to players in a particular geographical area.

composite—A reference to tennis rackets made from a combination of two or more materials; for example, one made from graphite and fiberglass.

Continental grip—A way of holding the racket so that the player does not have to change grips between the forehand and backhand strokes; the wrist is directly over the top of the grip.

cross strings—Strings running horizontally from one side of the racket head to the other.

crosscourt—A shot hit diagonally from one corner of the court to the opposite corner.

Davis Cup—An international team tennis event for male players.

deep—A reference to the area near the baseline.

default—The awarding of a match to one player or team because an opponent fails to appear or is not able to complete a match; synonym for forfeit.

deuce—A tie score at 40-40, and each tie thereafter in the same game.

deuce court—The right half of a player's court as that player faces the baseline.

dink—A shot hit with very little pace or depth.

double fault—Failure on both attempts to serve into the proper court.

doubles—A match played with four players.

down the line—A shot hit more or less parallel to the closest sideline.

drive—A groundstroke hit forcefully and deeply into an opponent's backcourt.

drop shot—A softly hit shot, usually having backspin, that barely clears the net and bounces twice before the opponent can get to it.

Eastern backhand grip— A grip in which the V formed by the thumb and index finger is above but slightly toward the left of the racket handle as a right-handed player prepares to hit a backhand.

Eastern forehand grip— A grip in which the V formed by the thumb and index finger is above but slightly toward the right of the racket handle as a right-handed player prepares to hit a forehand.

error—A point lost as a result of one player's mistake rather than the other player's good shot.

face—The flat hitting surface formed by the strings and the racket head.

fast—A reference to a tennis court surface on which the ball bounces low and moves rapidly toward or away from the hitter.

fault—Failure on an attempt to serve into the proper court.

Federation Cup—An international team tennis event for female players.

feed-in consolation—A tournament in which players who lose in the early rounds of a tournament reenter the championship draw and may finish as high as 5th place.

fiberglass—A somewhat flexible form of glass fibers used in some rackets.

finals—The match played to determine the winner of a tournament.

flat—A reference to a shot hit with little or no spin. Also a term used to describe tennis balls that have lost their firmness and resilience.

flexibility—How much a racket bends from head to shaft or from one side of the head to the other when contact with the ball is made.

follow-through—The part of the swinging motion after the ball has been hit.

forcing shot—A shot hit with enough pace or depth to force an opponent into a difficult return.

forehand—A stroke that a right-handed player hits on the right side of the body and a left-hander hits on the left side.

forfeit—The awarding of a match to one player or team because an opponent fails to appear or is not able to complete a match; synonym for default.

frame—The tennis racket, excluding the strings.

graphite—A man-made, carbon-based material 20 times stronger and stiffer than wood, often used in rackets.

grip—The manner in which a racket is held. Also, the part of the racket where it is held.

grommet—A small, round plastic sleeve in the frame, through which the strings pass.

groove—To hit shots in a patterned, disciplined, and consistent manner.

groundstroke—A shot that is hit with a forehand or backhand stroke after the ball has bounced on the court.

gut—Racket string made from beef or sheep intestines.

hacker—A person who does not play tennis well.

half volley—A shot hit just after the ball has bounced on the court; contact is made below knee level.

head—The upper part of the racket where the strings are attached.

head heavy— A reference to a racket whose balance point is more than 1/4 inch from the center (midpoint of the racket's length) toward the head.

head light— A reference to a racket whose balance point is more than 1/4 inch from the center (midpoint of the racket's length) toward the handle.

hitting surface—The flat surface formed by the strings.

holding serve—The server has won the game that he or she just served.

hook—A slang term meaning to cheat.

International Tennis Federation (ITF)—An organization that governs international amateur competition and has some jurisdiction over professional tennis.

invitational tournament—A tournament open only to players who have been invited to participate.

junior—A player 19 years old or younger.

Kevlar—A synthetic fiber used to strengthen tennis racket frames.

ladder tournament—A type of competition in which the names of participants are placed in a column; players can advance up the column (ladder) by challenging and defeating players whose names appear above their own.

let—A serve that hits the top of the net and lands in the proper service court. Also, an expression used to indicate that a point should be replayed for any of a number of other reasons.

linesperson—An official who is responsible for calling shots either in or out at either the baseline, service line, or center service line.

lob—A high, arching shot.

lob volley—A lob hit with a volley.

long—An informal expression used to indicate that a shot went out past the baseline.

love—An archaic but commonly used way to say zero in the tennis scoring system.

main strings—The vertical strings, running from the top to the bottom of the racket head.

match—Competition between two players in singles, four players in doubles, or between two teams, as when two school teams compete against each other.

match point—The stage of a match when a player can win the match by winning the next point. The term is used by spectators and television announcers during a match and by players after a match; it is not, or should not be, used by the umpire or players in calling out the score.

mixed doubles—Competition pairing a man and woman on one team against a man and woman on the other team.

net umpire—An official responsible for calling let serves.

no—An informal expression used by some players to call shots out.

no-ad—A scoring system in which a maximum of 7 points constitutes a game. For example, if the score is tied at 3 points for each player, the next player to win a point wins the game.

no man's land—The area of the court between the service line and the baseline. This area is usually considered a weak area from which to return shots during a rally.

not up—An expression used to indicate that a ball has bounced twice on the same side before being hit.

nylon—A strong, synthetic material commonly used for racket strings.

open tennis—Competition open to amateur and professional players.

out—A call indicating that a shot has bounced outside a boundary line.

overgrip—A one-piece grip that slides over the original racket grip.

overhead smash—A hard, powerful stroke hit from an over-the-head racket position.

pace—The velocity with which a ball is hit; or the velocity of the ball.

passing shot—A groundstroke hit out of the reach of an opponent at the net.

percentage shot—The safest, most effective shot hit in a particular situation.

placement—A winning shot hit to an open area of the court; or the area of the court to which a ball is targeted.

playing pro—A person who makes a living playing tennis.

poaching—When a doubles player at the net cuts in front of the partner to hit a volley.

point penalty—A system in which a player may be penalized points, games, or even matches for improper conduct.

power zone—The area of the racket's hitting surface that produces controlled power with no vibration (see also *sweet spot*).

pro set—A match that is completed when one player or team has won at least 8 games and is ahead by at least 2 games.

professional (pro)—A person who plays or teaches tennis for money.

pusher—A type of player who is consistent, but who hits with very little pace.

put-away—A shot that is literally put away (out of reach) from an opponent.

qualifying round—A series of matches played to determine which players will be added to a tournament field.

rally—An exchange of shots.

ready position—The position in which a player stands while waiting for a shot.

receiver—The player to whom a serve is hit.

referee—An official responsible for supervising all competition during a tournament.

retriever—A type of player, much like the pusher, who gets everything back but does not play aggressively.

round robin—A type of competition in which all participants compete against each other in a series of matches. The player or team finishing the competition with the best win-loss percentage is the winner.

rush—To move toward the net following a forcing shot.

second—An informal expression used by some players to indicate that the first serve is out.

serve—The shot used to put the ball into play at the beginning of a point.

server—The player who begins a point with a serve.

service break—The loss of a game by the player serving.

service court—Either of two alternating areas into which the ball must be served; its boundaries are the net, the center line, the service line, and the singles sideline.

service line—The line that is parallel to, and 21 feet from, the net.

set—The part of a match that is completed when a player or team has won at least 6 games and is ahead by at least 2 games.

set point—The stage of a set when a player or team can win the set by winning the next point.

shaft—The part of the racket between the head and the grip.

sideline—The boundary line that runs from the net to the baseline. The singles sidelines are closer to the center of the court than the doubles sidelines.

single elimination tournament—A type of competition in which players' names are drawn and placed on lines in a tournament bracket roster. Matches are played between players whose names appear on connected bracket lines. Players who win advance to the next round of competition; those who lose a match are eliminated from competition.

slice—To hit a ball with sidespin, like the spin of a top.

slow—A description of a court surface on which the ball bounces and slows down after the bounce.

split sets—An expression used to indicate that two players or teams have each won a set.

straight sets—A reference to winning a match without losing a set.

stroke—The manner in which a ball is hit (forehand, backhand, volley, etc.).

sweet spot—The exact place on the racket face that produces controlled power with no vibration (see also *power zone*).

synthetic—A type of racket string made from specially designed nylon.

take two—An expression meaning that the server should repeat both service attempts.

teaching pro—A person who teaches people to play tennis and is paid for the service. Teaching pros are usually distinguished from playing pros, although some professionals teach and play for money.

throat—The part of the racket just below the head.

tiebreaker—A method of completing a set when both players or teams have won 6 games.

titanium—A strong, lustrous, white metal element used in the construction of some rackets.

topspin—Bottom-to-top rotation on a ball, like a car wheel going forward.

touch—The ability to hit a variety of precision shots.

umpire—A person responsible for officiating a match between two players or teams.

unforced error—A point lost with absolutely no pressure having been exerted by the opponent.

United States Tennis Association (USTA)—A national, noncommercial membership organization that promotes tennis in a variety of ways.

vibration dampener—A rubber or plastic device inserted at the base of the racket strings (near the throat) to reduce the vibration of the strings upon impact with the ball.

volley—A shot hit before the ball bounces on the court.

Western grip—A way of holding the racket in which the wrist is positioned directly behind the handle.

wide—An expression used by some players to indicate a shot went out beyond a sideline.

widebody—A description of a racket frame with a very wide head.

Wimbledon—A tournament in England, generally considered to be the most prestigious in the world.

World Tennis Association (WTA)—An organization consisting of the world's leading female professional players.

yoke—The part of the racket immediately below the head; the upper part of the shaft; the throat.

ABOUT THE AUTHOR

Jim Brown served for five years as the editor of *Tennis Industry* magazine and is now executive editor of the *Penn State Sports Medicine Newsletter*. He began playing tennis more than 40 years ago and has experience as a teaching professional, a college instructor and coach, a city program director, a writer and publisher, a consultant, and a clinician. He has represented the United States Tennis Association; the American Alliance for Health, Physical Education, Recreation and Dance; and the President's Council on Physical Fitness and Sports in clinics throughout the United States and Mexico.

Jim has written, coauthored, or edited 8 books and more than 100 articles on a variety of health and physical education topics. Jim received a PhD in health and physical education from the University of North Texas in 1971. In 1991, he was inducted into the McNeese State University Hall of Fame. Jim lives in Atlanta, GA, with his wife, Katherine.

*You'll find
other outstanding
tennis resources at*

www.humankinetics.com

In the U.S. call

1-800-747-4457

Australia 08 8277 1555
Canada 1-800-465-7301
Europe .... +44 (0) 113 278 1708
New Zealand 09-523-3462

HUMAN KINETICS
The Premier Publisher for Sports & Fitness
P.O. Box 5076 • Champaign, IL 61825-5076 USA